Foreward

A book should not be just something to read it should be something to possess. May this book become your prized possession. May it be a source of answers, while allowing God, the creator, to be **the** source of your answers.

Testimonials

"After reading this book, my head was all full of WOW! " - Becky B.

"Congratulations! Hope you sell a million of them. It's a monumental accomplishment." - Ruth C.

"I am about three fourths of the way in and I can't explain to you how positive I feel . . .." – Derrick S.

Acknowledgements

Thanks to the books, newspapers, websites, tapes, magazines, DVD's, etc., that I've received answers from. Portions of many of these and many others contributed to this book.

Thanks to all the people who contributed to my experiences that led to this book, especially the Stand, Reach and Edge team, Sue, Bettie, Ray, Cindy, and my life coach, rubye(rubye prefers the lowercase r.). To the Chanhassen American Legion for allowing me those wonderful experiences. And a special thanks to Mom, Dad, my four sisters and eight brothers for all those experiences.

And a very special thank you to my life partner Becky, for contributing to the consciousness shift in me while creating this book. To my children, Kristie, Bonnie and Ryan, and my grandchildren Brooke, Mackenzie, Damien, Isabella Rose. And Becky's family, for helping to make my consciousness shift more purposeful, powerful and enjoyable.

To God, for enjoying sharing this experience.

Contents

Foreward 3
Testimonials 3
Acknowledgements 4
Getting Ready 9
    Doubt 13
    Ready Or Not 16
    Trusting My Gut 20
    How? 24
    The Jr. Honor Guard 26
    Feelings Are Messages 31
    Normal Or Natural 31
    My Struggle 33
    False Beliefs 36
    The Formula 38
Your Body 41
    The Beginning 42
    The Split 44
    A Consciousness Shift 47
    God Is In You 51
    Breathe 55
Your Soul 59
    Experiencing Our Life Plan 60

The Creation Of ICURY 61
Your Owned Feelings 64
Our Soul Knows 66
Be Mindless 67
My Plan 68
Bringing Focus 70
Finding Your Passion 72
Your Mind 75
A New Way Of Thinking 77
Out Of The Blue 81
Feeling Good 83
Our Path 85
Storing Experiences 87
Attracting 89
You Create Experiences 93
Ask And Receive 93
You Cause God's Feelings 96
Think By Chance Or By Choice 98
Creating Thought 102
You, A Creator 106
Experiences 121
Living Consciously 139
Ask And You Shall Receive 153

You Are A Creation Machine 163
Defining World Peace 183
Seeking The Experience 185
Defining God 188
Man Is God Made 190
God is Man made 192
Consciousness Shift Summary 209
Body 209
Soul 209
Mind 210
Body, Soul, Mind 211
Unity and Oneness 211
Harmony 212
Consciousness 212
Experiences 213
Source 213
You 213
Massive Shift 214
Birthing World Peace: 215
Book Orders 218
Disclaimer 220

We Have

Forgotten

Who We

Really

Are

Getting Ready

Are you ready for world peace? Are you ready for supreme happiness, bliss, utter joy and euphoria? Would you be willing to participate in making all of that happen, especially if you could do that at a pace that you are comfortable with?

If world peace happened today, would the world be ready? The chaos we are currently experiencing on earth allows us to observe that the world is about as far from peace as it's ever been. That's good. Here's why! For man to fully appreciate the experience of world peace, man needs to experience the absence of it, such as the chaos we are now experiencing. In other words, we've experienced the bad, so that we'll appreciate the good when we experience that.

Our world is feeling bad while we wait for peace to happen. How many of us were brought into this world to wait for peace? I believe we are all here to create peace. How much better would everyone feel if they were creating world peace instead of waiting for it. We wait in desperation while we could be creating in inspiration.

Given the choice, humans on earth would vote for peace. That is, if a vote is all that was needed. Would those same humans vote for world peace if they knew what was needed from each of them to make world peace happen? Would you?

We know the absence of world peace. We know it intimately since we are experiencing it. No human on earth has ever experienced the opposite, the presence of world peace, and therefore no human knows the experience of world peace.

Nothing is more stimulating to humans than the prospect of peace. Imagine how it would feel to be alive, on this earth, in that moment when world peace is created. Imagine too how you would feel if you helped make that happen. I get goose bumps just thinking about it.

Draw a picture in your mind's eye of what world peace would look like, not just for you but for everyone. Since no human on earth has ever experienced world peace, you have no one to go to to find out what that would be like. Start drawing the picture of planet earth experiencing world peace for the very first time. It makes you wonder, doesn't it. What would a picture of world peace really look like? It boggles the mind to think of all of the possibilities, the opportunities and the changes we will experience.

No human knows what world peace will be like and yet every human wants it, instinctually. Many don't care what peace will look like or be like; they just simply want it. And they want it now!

Do you want to be part of the generation that finally makes world peace happen? What would you be willing to do or to give up to experience world peace in your lifetime? Would you be willing to give away every thing you own, including your money, your house, your car, if that is what it would take? That is not what it will take. If world peace was a certainty, what would you be willing to sacrifice to attain it? How important is it to you, your loved ones, your country and your world?

If you haven't dreamt about world peace or about making it happen, maybe you haven't been dreaming big enough. One thing is certain. When you dream about making world peace happen, you are not dreaming too small. Making world peace happen will be a monumental accomplishment for all of us.

Sound impossible? It did for me. That is, until I found out what it will take. I've moved from impossible to not just possible but probable. ICURY is my sharing that shift with you.

The definition of world peace surprised me. It may surprise you too. Evidence of achieving world peace would mean we would be living in a world where the following are guaranteed.

1. *The basic needs of everyone are met, guaranteed.*

2. *Everyone has the opportunity to go higher, guaranteed.*

These are the only two requirements God says are needed for us to experience world peace. (We will discuss *basic needs* and *go higher* later in this book.) And God also says that a change in human consciousness is what is needed to achieve these two requirements.

For centuries, humans have been thinking, talking, singing and writing about peace but not achieving it. The observable truth is that it is going to take more than just thinking, talking, singing and writing to make it happen. It will take human involvement. To what degree are you willing to get involved to make it happen?

What the world has been doing is not working. A different solution is needed. If anyone on earth had used the correct solution before, we would have world peace now. What we've been doing for thousands of years has not served us well.

Get ready for a change. Lots of change. But don't be too surprised if it's not the change you expected. Think about all of the changes you believe are needed to make world peace happen. Then, while reading ICURY, notice how your thoughts are in or out of alignment with what you read. Remember that what we've been doing has not and is not working. Change is needed. We can or will change, in very enjoyable ways, to make it happen.

You have started on your path to becoming an instrument of peace. This journey will be immensely enjoyable.

Doubt

Everyone is either an instrument of peace or is an instrument of the absence of peace. Which one are you? Being an instrument of peace means you are affecting peace. The observable condition of the world indicates that people on earth are affecting the absence of peace. If the opposite were true, we would be experiencing world peace today.

Does it excite you to think that you could actually help affect world peace? Before you are done reading this book, you will see how we will make that happen. You are about to experience what will likely be the biggest change of your life. Be encouraged by witnessing others noticing your excitement and wanting that for themselves.

Imagine being able to honestly say, "I was instrumental in creating the world peace which we are enjoying today." Imagine how you would feel saying that, living that, being that. Do you want to experience that change as it occurs in you, your family, your friends, the whole world? Imagine finding the solution in this book.

How would you feel if you found out what is really needed for humans to experience world peace? Not just knowing what world peace is but actually discovering the answer to experiencing world peace! It's one thing to talk about and know what world peace is but it's an entirely different thing to experience world peace. Experiencing world peace is actually living it!

Would you believe that you could receive the answer to world peace, out of the blue, like I did? Would you believe the answer could come to you, just because you were asking God for it? Would you accept that you had received this all-important answer when it arrived? Would you believe that was possible?

So let's say you received the answer and believed it was true. Let's also say you believed the answer to the degree that you thought you had to act on it. It was too important to you to know it, and then not act on it. You thought about it constantly and the more you thought about it the more you felt compelled to share the answer. You thought a book might be the best way to spread the word. You started writing the book, for days, for weeks, for months, even for years. And, the more you wrote, the more the answers came to you.

But all the while you were writing, the issue of worthiness kept coming to mind. Who am I to think I can write a book on experiencing world peace? Who am I to think I can ask God, the creator, questions and get answers? Who am I to think that the creator chose me to do this? And if God didn't choose me, then why was I getting so many answers? Was it because I was the only person asking the questions or the only one receiving the answers or the only one ready for the answers or the only one acting on the answers?

Notice all of the doubt in what I was doing and thinking. As I was writing, I was asking more questions and receiving more answers and in the process removing more doubt.

My hope is that I can do the same for you. It could have been you writing this book. It could have been you asking the questions and receiving the answers. You can do everything that I have done and more.

You will likely question many parts of this book. That is good. If all you get out of this book is to question God about what is said in it, then you are already participating in asking. If you also receive answers to your questions, then you are also consciously participating in the receiving part of ask and you shall receive.

We were all given free will. You have free will to ask, or not ask, God. You also have free will, after you've asked, to allow answers or not.

Ready Or Not

God knows if you are ready for an answer or not. This book will not answer that question for you because the answer is in your soul and only your soul knows your path. I had to learn this lesson early in this process. I thought I could ask a question and immediately receive an answer. I did not know that sometimes I'd get an answer quickly and other times it would take days, weeks and at times, even longer. I didn't know that I wasn't ready for some of the answers I was asking for.

Some of the answers I received helped me learn how to become ready for the following answers. This was another area where doubt played a big part in how soon I readied myself for those answers. Undoubtedly you too will doubt some of what you read here. You will even come to doubt some of your own doubts.

Many people believe that God is very, very important in their lives but then don't listen to God. Do you listen to man more than you listen to God? Do you listen to teachers, the media, parents and grandparents, ministers and everyone else more than you listen to God?

Observe who you listen to most. Compare that to how much you listen to God. That is your observable truth. Would you say all of the people you listen to are more important than God? Or, is God more important to listen to than all of them? Do you doubt you can listen to God? Do you doubt you can ask questions of and receive answers from God?

What percentage of everything that is in your mind came from people and what percentage came directly from God? Should we be listening to man or should we be listening to God? Observe the condition of earth today. Would we be better served to change who we are listening to?

What would your mind be filled with today if you would have been taught to listen to God when you were very young. How different would you be today? Would you be willing to, be open to listening to God, if you knew you could do that? Would you and the world be better today?

My name is Ron. I'm just a regular guy with a job, a family, a life partner, 66 years of experiences and a passion for experiencing world peace. More than anything else, I'd like to see my children and grandchildren experience world peace. That means I don't want them to simply read about world peace, hear about world peace or think about world peace. I want them to experience world peace. Many people have told me that they think that achieving world peace is impossible and that it will not happen.

Just the thought that experiencing world peace might be possible was very motivational and helped me through the process of writing this book. As you'll read, this hasn't been a small or easy task. I wanted to quit many times and just agree with those who said world peace was impossible. If you have thoughts of giving up, consider that there are many more of us now working on this together.

Mankind has a long history of focusing on thoughts and actions while ignoring feelings. Each generation learned from the previous generation and it has continued for thousands of years. We therefore have a history of giving focus to our mind and body and ignoring our soul.

What are your thoughts and feelings about war? There is a big difference between how you feel vs what you think. You **think** your **thoughts**! You **experience** your **feelings**! Many people know their thoughts about war but pay little attention to their feelings about it. If you know your feelings, they are your truth. If you don't know your feelings, they are still your truth. Your feelings never lie. You can always, always trust them. Some refer to this as **trusting your gut**, as your gut is where many feelings are experienced.

On the other hand, all of the thoughts in your mind are thoughts that you have placed there. They are not necessarily truth and cannot always be trusted. Those thoughts came from numerous sources and some are true. You can, if you wish, decide to trust all of your thoughts, even though that may not serve you well.

Trusting My Gut

Trusting my gut served me well in Vietnam during my fourteen-month participation in that war in 1970-1971. Then I did not understand that trusting my gut was actually trusting my feelings. I also did not understand that those feelings that I experienced were actually delivered to my body from somewhere else. I had the mistaken belief that the feelings just occurred in my body but gave no thought to whether that was the truth about feelings or not. I later learned that **in my body** is where I experience them, only after they are delivered from that somewhere else.

In Vietnam I just knew trusting my gut as something inside of me that I noticed on occasion. Most times when I noticed a feeling, that feeling in my gut alerted me to something, usually something I should avoid, be careful of, or not trust. When it occurred, I paid attention, and that helped me and those around me to stay alive. I was starting to experience the importance of feelings but I was not yet having conscious thought about those feelings or where they came from.

Not everyone was as fortunate as me. Many died, on both sides. It was part of war, I thought. I had to accept that, I thought. It affected me but it didn't stick with me nearly as much as the soldiers who killed themselves. As Army Military Policemen, our job included writing up the initial reports at suicide scenes. As I saw it, at those scenes, the soldier was now dead and the family was left to cope with that. I didn't think the family should also have to cope with the idea that their son committed suicide. I therefore never used the word suicide when writing those police reports.

Those soldier suicides really bothered me. I became very angry. I was angry at the women who wrote the Dear John letters that those soldiers were reading at the time. How could any woman possibly do that to a guy who was already under more stress than a human should have to endure? Why couldn't they wait until he got home where he wouldn't have a rifle in his lap when he found out about the relationship breakup? Today's military also has female soldiers serving and receiving Dear Jane letters from their loved ones.

I was angry at the military for not having something in place to keep this from happening, at least less often. Why didn't they take the weapons away from the soldiers, briefly, when the soldiers got the mail that finally caught up with them? Or why didn't they have something in place so the spouse, or girlfriend, could notify the military and then the military could break the news to the soldier while he didn't have a rifle in his lap?

I carried that anger for much of my life. Many years after the war I became active with other veterans issues. I continued to read about soldier and veteran suicides and how that statistic was worse than most any other category.

Years later, during my three terms as Commander of an American Legion Post, I had the opportunity to meet with military officials and learn first-hand what was being done for current military members regarding suicides. I also met with Department of Veterans Affairs officials to share and discuss what was being done or what could be done for veterans no longer active in the military. It appeared every single thing they were doing was having an impact but far too many suicides were still occurring.

This went on for years while I learned more about suicides, in general, which were not that different. Far too many of them were also occurring. More studies were being done. I did a lot of reading and research. Somewhere in this whole mess of things the answer finally came to me that the only true solution to reducing suicides was to have world peace. World peace would not just reduce veteran and military suicides but all suicides.

This answer did not come from out of the blue like so many answers before. No, this one arrived accompanied with a strong gut level feeling like I had not experienced before. Not only did I think it was the right answer, I knew, with feeling, that it was truth.

I was convinced it was the solution I had been looking for for so very long. It was a relief to me, to my system, especially my stress level. My gut was telling me this was it. My feelings were telling me that this was truly the answer I was looking for the past forty years.

But it didn't feel complete. Something was missing. I had the answer, or did I? I had the answer that experiencing world peace would reduce suicides but I didn't have the answer on how to attain world peace.

How?

World peace seemed so far away, so impossible. No way could we ever have world peace. It was never going to happen, I thought. How could we ever stop all wars much less have world peace? I had experienced the end of several wars in my lifetime but that didn't seem to bring us any closer to world peace. It was going to take more than just ending wars.

From my view, the whole world was in chaos. Even nature appeared to be in chaos. No matter where I looked there was chaos. But if ever world peace was needed, it was now. It seemed everything was moving away from world peace instead of towards it.

Because my passion of finding a solution to reducing suicides had also become an obsession, I wasn't going to quit now. At least so I thought. During the long process of getting to where I am now, I had discovered that when I thought about something long enough, hard enough, with enough energy, an answer would show up. I continued to do a lot of reading, as a source of God's answers to my questions.

I had discovered that **ask and you shall receive** did not work for me when I asked for money or other material things. But it did work for me when I asked for answers to questions. When I asked, it wasn't long before an answer came - from somewhere, out of the blue. Asking questions, with sincerity and feeling always resulted in receiving an answer in some form sooner or later. For me, there was definitely something to the **ask and you shall receive** idea.

I had also, unintentionally, placed myself in a box. Over the years, I had quite often said to others, sometimes flippantly, "Nobody wants peace more than a veteran." I believed that, but that belief alone did not bring us any closer to world peace. One day I simply asked myself, *"If it is true that nobody wants peace more than a veteran, and you are a veteran, then what are you doing about it?"* It hit me right between the eyes! I said it! I believed it!

But what was I doing about it? It did not matter what other veterans **weren't doing** about it. It was **me** telling others that nobody wants peace more than a veteran. It was me saying it, believing it, and not doing anything about it. That was a rather rude awakening.

I started giving more thought to what world peace actually was. After all, it had to be defined before it could be achieved. I remembered the protesters yelling, swearing and spitting at us when we returned from Vietnam. They claimed to be for peace but protested against the war. The observable truth was that they did not get us any closer to world peace.

In many cases, they simply added to the violence that was already going on. They had the mistaken belief that stopping war would result in peace. One could observe that they did not get world peace from their protesting. Standing against war does not give one world peace, even when a war is stopped. **Standing for** something <u>assists</u> in achieving something but **standing against** something <u>resists</u> in achieving something.

The Jr. Honor Guard

Some of the protesters lost family members in the war. Thinking about the military families, especially the children who lost a parent was especially emotional. It seemed about as unfair as life could be.

Joining the protesters was a way for the relatives of the fallen soldiers to take a stand against war. It made the adults feel better, if only briefly. The children were there with the protesters and they were now experiencing what it's like to stand against something. Being with such angry people could not have felt good. These and many other thoughts were what helped me continue following my passion.

One of the benefits of my being an American Legion Post Commander was that I was given a lot of opportunities to do projects of my choosing. My favorite project, by far, was the Jr. Honor Guard project. Before forming the Jr. Honor Guard, I watched the American Legion Color Guard lead many parades. I watched the audience stand, cheer, applaud and shout thank you. It was obvious people wanted to show their appreciation for what the soldiers and veterans had done.

But I couldn't do that for the soldiers who were currently in uniform. I had no way to get soldiers into the parade so the crowd could show their appreciation directly to them. I couldn't get the deployed soldiers home, much less into the parade.

But what about the soldier's children? That's when the idea of the Jr. Honor Guard came to me. The Jr. Honor Guard was made up of children of deployed parents marching in the parade. This allowed the community to show their appreciation for what they were going through and how much the community cared.

That first year we had sixty eight children of deployed parents marching right behind the American Legion Color Guard. Each child was given a U.S. flag, dog tags with their name on it, a T shirt honoring their deployed parent and a certificate of appreciation. Following the parade, each child was given a CD with parade film to send to their deployed parent. Each child received a buffet meal along with their favorite ice cream treat as well as a pizza certificate so the child could treat their deployed parent to a pizza when they returned home.

I had the pleasure of marching with the children and enjoyed the most emotional event I have ever experienced. I watched the children as the crowd cheered so very loud, forceful and with such emotion. I watched the crowd stand, wave, cheer, applaud, yell thank you, and even shed tears which was beyond my greatest expectations. To watch people in wheel chairs struggle to stand up to honor those kids was beyond my belief. I tear up right now writing about it.

I also had the pleasure of watching the little wide-eyed babies in strollers, pushed by a parent or guardian, with the little flags attached. Small children proudly held and waved little flags that they now treasured. Middle aged children, especially the boys, waved their flags but also proudly showed off their dog tags.

The teenagers were especially affected. They did not know the magnitude of support they had in the community until then. To watch the tears run down their faces as they watched the tears on the faces of many in the audience was so tremendously healing for all. I fought the tears for a bit and then realized the crowd was watching the children so I just let it happen. It was also a healing experience for me.

Three local TV stations filmed the Jr. Honor Guard in the parade for the evening news. I recorded all three and had tears every time I watched them over the following years. I used those strong emotional reminders whenever I wanted to feel really good.

The feelings I experienced in that parade were the strongest feelings I had ever experienced. Each time I watched the recordings I'd re-experience those feelings nearly at that same strong level. Each time I watched it, I was more convinced that I was on the right path; that what I had done was the right thing.

With such strong feelings, how could one not wonder about feelings in general? I did! I had plenty of opportunity to re-experience those feelings every time I watched those recordings. The feelings that each of us experienced in the parade and each time I watched those recordings came from somewhere. But where?

What and where is that **thing** that sends the feelings? This question **came** to me and before long the answer **came** too. Those feelings were coming from that place where my life plan is stored.

Soon thereafter I read that feelings are the language of the soul. I asked and received my answer, and this time it was through a book. I learned that I could ask by simply saying the question. I also was learning that I could ask by simply thinking the question. Either way, God, the creator, was listening.

The question became, was I listening when God answered? Was I being mindful of other ways the creator might be answering my questions? After much practicing, it became evident that answers were arriving in many different forms. Sometimes the answers came directly into the mind, out of the blue as they say. Sometimes it was words in a song, reading a book, newspaper or billboards. Sometimes it was hearing someone say it or sing it. I could always tell if it was an answer for me. When it was really an answer for me, it was accompanied by a good feeling. I was learning to trust my feelings even more. Now I was getting answers to my questions and I was getting feelings as messages to confirm them.

Feelings Are Messages

Feelings are how the soul speaks to us. Feelings are sent as messages. Each feeling that people experience in their bodies is a message. The message tells the person that he or she is on the right path or not. If the feeling is good, then you are on a good path for you.

Feelings are always messages but you may not be paying attention in each and every moment of your life. Do you treat each message from your soul as being important? Do you react to each feeling as though it was an answer from the soul? A new feeling is sent to your body for each new experience.

Normal Or Natural

So far, you've read more questions than answers! Today, it's likely your **normal** is to ask more questions of others than of God. It is, however, in your **nature** to ask more questions of God than from others. When **normally doing something** becomes **naturally doing something,** you will be asking questions of the source that best serves you. Many more humans could be asking questions of God and be assured of honest answers.

The soul uses the same language, feelings, to send messages to every human body. It does not matter if you speak English, French or Spanish. All messages come from the soul through the language of feeling. It's a very simple system. Feelings are your very own built in truth detector and you have free will to use it or not.

Experience a **good** feeling. Next, experience a **bad** feeling. Be grateful for having experienced **both** feelings. Know that the **bad** feeling is there to remind you of the difference, the **good** feeling.

The information in this book is not about my trying to change your consciousness. It is about how I learned to change my consciousness.

God said a change in consciousness is required before humans can experience peace. Are you willing to change your consciousness if that would allow you to experience peace? My passion is to affect a global consciousness shift.

My Struggle

I struggle with knowing so much more than I did before and yet not always being able to add action to that which I have learned. How does one motivate another to take a sustainable action when one has not motivated oneself to do the same? I've learned a lot and taken a lot of action in the process but it is a much slower process than I expected. Everyone is in a different state of readiness, to move to a higher energy level, so everyone will move at their own pace according to the soul path they are on. I am moving at my own pace as I am also on my soul path.

Growing up in the 50's on a farm in central Minnesota, the oldest son in a family of thirteen kids, was quite an experience. Fifty some years later, I look back in wonder. Many times throughout that journey, I encountered experiences where something on the farm broke down, a tool, a tractor or piece of machinery. No matter what broke, I'd either fix it and go on, or ask Dad what to do. He'd often say, *"Well, fix it!"* To which I'd respond, *"I don't know how."* To which he'd respond, *"Well, figure it out."*

What I did not know at that young age was that I could **Ask** God. **Ask and you shall receive** was something I heard about but it was never explained to me in the way that I understand it today. What I find fascinating now is that I did not fully know how to **Ask and you shall receive** but I was doing it anyway. Did you know that you are doing it too?

As a child I would have understood it to mean that I would have had to physically ask, by saying the words out loud, and asking in that way. *"How do I fix the broken field cultivator?"* I was also under the impression that the only way to get an answer was to hear it with my ears. In other words, I would have actually heard a voice or voices saying the answer. Everyone around me would have heard it too. I also knew that others weren't doing it that way or I would have heard them asking and I would have heard their answers too.

Can a person, a human being, figure this out? When you attempt to figure something out, aren't you asking your mind for an answer? Can you place an image of a problem in your mind and start wondering how to solve the problem?

I had only one place to go. I could go directly to God. Ask and you shall receive produced the contents of this book. God and I were co-creators of this book just as you and God are co-creators and will be co-creators in the creation of world peace.

Taking on a goal of writing a book which, when read and followed by enough humans, would create world peace was a huge undertaking. I had no one to ask what to include in this book. There also was no book I could read that explained how to do what I was about to do. Humans have attempted many things in the name of peace and the observable truth about the non-peaceful condition of the world is that what we have done in the past and what we are currently doing is not working.

There is no school on earth that will teach you what you are going to learn while reading this book. Does that scare you or make you think it isn't true? Keep reading and you'll find out how to know without doubt what your truth is. In knowing this you will never again have to rely on anyone else for your truth.

Achieving world peace is not something I can do alone. I don't pretend to know all the answers. I do know that I've been given many answers that I did not have earlier in my life. I also know that I've received many answers that I do not fully understand, yet. Many answers raise even more questions which I have not yet taken the time to ask and receive answers to.

My consciousness of who I am has increased dramatically since I started work on this book. Humans have been changing circumstances for centuries in an attempt to achieve peace. Observable truth shows that hasn't and isn't working. God says we don't need a change of circumstances, but rather, a change of consciousness, to achieve world peace. How can we change our consciousness? Keep reading and you'll learn how I changed mine.

False Beliefs

For centuries people believed the earth was flat. That was their truth. Someone proved that that was not true. People who believed the earth was flat then chose a different belief. Based on the new facts, they now believe the earth is round. Take notice that this example shows that those people did not change in body or soul, but only changed their minds. By changing their minds, they changed their beliefs. They now believe the earth is round. Take notice that nothing around those people changed either, in the sense that the world did not change from being flat to being round. Only what was in the mind changed. Like others, this truth is observable.

People observed a round earth. They could no longer believe the earth was flat as that was no longer their truth. Notice that, for all these people, the truth in each of their minds changed. The truth before they found out the earth was round was that the earth was flat. It was their truth at that time. After they found out the earth was round, they added that truth to their mind.

They then had two differing truths about the shape of the earth. Both truths were, and are, in their mind. One was a truth that was true for them at one time in their life and the other was true for them at another time in their life. It is a rather major belief change to move from a flat earth belief to a round earth belief.

For centuries people went about their daily lives thinking and believing the earth was flat. In most people's lives they simply did not give it further thought. They thought it was truth and truth could not, and would not, change.

What if something similar has gone on in our lifetime that could be just as earth changing? What if you learned a new truth that could and would change the earth and, indeed, the whole world. Would you be open to and welcome that new truth?

What if believing that new truth moved you closer to experiencing world peace? Would you be ready for that new belief and place that new belief to your mind?

My hope is that this book will lead you to go direct to God. God does not listen more to me than to any of you. God listens to all. Just ask and you too will receive. God answers all.

The Formula

In one of his *'Conversations With God'* books, the author, Neale Donald Walsch, quotes God as saying, *"This one simple change - seeking and finding peace within - could, were it undertaken by everyone, end all wars, eliminate conflict, prevent prejudice, and bring the world to everlasting peace. There is no other formula necessary, or possible. World peace is a personal thing. What is needed is not a change in circumstance, but a change in consciousness."*

Notice the sentence, *"There is no other formula necessary, or possible."* In other words, there is no other **possible** formula for world peace. This is the **only** formula that will bring about world peace.

Notice, how, in this chapter, my beliefs and my consciousness changed. In the chapters that follow, it will change even more. So will yours.

The Wondrously Magnificent Human Body

Your Body

This chapter takes you through a consciousness shift about your body. Notice as you attract that shift. It will guide you on your path to becoming an instrument of peace.

In my computer software experiences, I dove into the bits and bytes of the microprocessor, enjoying the 0's and 1's that make up computer processing. I didn't know I'd be enjoying it until I started going deep into that subject. The computer is an amazing machine that has now become a large part of my life.

It was many years before I started paying attention to my body to that same degree of detail, my trillions of cells, with each having sensors that are an important part of my life. Each individual 0 or 1 has an important job to do in every computer, iPad, and cell phone, just as each individual cell has an important job to do in each of our bodies. But I didn't know any of that until I started going deep into that subject, what some call deep thinking.

The human body is a wondrously magnificent creation.

Are you aware that each and every cell in your body has its own consciousness? Every one of the more than 55 trillion cells that make up my body is a point of consciousness. Consciousness, according to one dictionary, means the state of being conscious, awareness of one's own existence, sensations, thoughts and surroundings, full activity of the mind and senses.

The Beginning

In that moment when we were conceived, this is what happened. The ovum from our mom met up with the sperm from our dad and they got together to form the first cell of our bodies.

That cell took the DNA from the ovum cell and took the DNA from the sperm cell and combined them into a new DNA set. That cell then changed a small portion of the combined DNA to make it unique to each of us. How that cell changed the DNA I do not know but that cell knew. That cell then made the changed DNA the DNA of the new cell. Amazing! That's how each of us was started.

That DNA, my DNA, was a new creation. It is and always will be different from every other human DNA on earth. Even in that very first cell, of me, I was different. I was, at that point, a new creation, the beginning of a new, wondrously magnificent, human body. Each of us was, and is!

How did that sperm and that ovum know how to get together and how to create a new cell out of themselves? And then how did that new cell know that it should take the DNA from the sperm and combine it with the DNA from the ovum.

How did that new cell know that it had to change the combined DNA into something unique so that it did not match any of the other seven billion people already on earth?

That first cell knew to do all that. Mom and dad did not tell the cell to do those things. That cell knew. Mom and dad put the ovum and sperm in close proximity to each other and then the cell took over. The cell even knew that it needed to create cells to connect to the inside of mom to get food to feed my body as I was being created. That first cell knew that it would be building my entire body. It knew how to do that too. It knew what to do first. It knew what to do next. The cell not only had to have a consciousness but a God consciousness in order to do all that. Only God knows the DNA of every human being that has ever lived.

The Split

When that first cell of my body started building my body, and split into many other cells, which cell was the first cell that started building my heart? How many cells of the heart were built when they decided, or knew, to start my heart beating? And which cells of my heart knew how to keep the heart beating, about 2 1/2 billion times in a lifetime?

When I was conceived, I started as a single cell. I am now made up of trillions of cells. I was born with approximately 7 trillion cells. As a full grown adult, I am now made up of approximately 55 trillion cells. They all work in harmony and unity to keep my body running. They perform millions of functions every second to do what they were created to do.

How does God do nothing and yet leave nothing undone? Such as it is with building your body, you do nothing and yet nothing is left undone.

Every human body is made up of trillions of cells and they all get along harmoniously with each other. There are only seven billion humans on earth and yet we don't get along harmoniously with each other. Those cells listen to God and they get along with each other. Would we all get along together if we all listened to God?

People
- About seven billion on earth
- Listen to other people
- Do not get along harmoniously

Cells of the body
- About fifty trillion in each body
- Listen to God
- Get along harmoniously

People should change who they listen to.

Imagine if our cells acted like people, some fighting about this and some fighting about that. Imagine if our cells decided to fight amongst themselves, like maybe the cells in one eye fighting with the cells in the other eye. What if the cells in one of our fingers got angry with the cells of another finger? What if some cells decided to have one of our ears start flapping? We are fortunate that the cells of our wondrously magnificent bodies get along with each other harmoniously.

What if the cells of your skin decided to no longer be your skin? It has happened and is happening! It took you more than a second to read this sentence. During that time, over 400 of your skin cells left your body. Did you select the ones that left? Over a million skin cells are replaced on the human body every hour. Our entire skin is replaced once a month. Generic material is replaced every six weeks. How do the cells know to do that?

Scientists have proven this but you still may not believe it. You may not like it, as it seems rather gross to have parts of you sprinkled like bread crumbs wherever you go. But, it happens and keeps happening and you have no control over it. It is simply your wondrously magnificent body doing what it was created to do. Imagine too, that by age seven, every single cell in your entire body, that you were born with, has been replaced by a new one. They all have that knowingness.

You don't have to tell the body, *"Go fix that finger I just cut."* It just knows! How did the cells know to build the lungs with an oxygen extracting surface the size of a tennis court? How did the cells know to build the lungs that size? How do your cells know how, where and when to make goose bumps? How about tears in your eyes? How about the blood circulation system, the brain, and all of our senses? How did they know how to build instinct and human nature into our bodies? I've built many things in my life but I have no idea how I'd go about building instinct or human nature into anything.

In 2016, a Japanese scientist at the Tokyo Institute of Technology won the Nobel Peace Prize in medicine. He was cited for "brilliant experiments" that illuminated autophagy in which cells gobble up damaged or worn out pieces of themselves. He showed how a cell can dispose of and recycle its garbage. The cell even knows how and when to do that. Another of many examples of God consciousness in each of our cells, of God consciousness in our entire body.

A Consciousness Shift

As you read this, you are developing a new consciousness about the consciousness of every cell in your body. In doing so, you created a change in your consciousness. You know that your body keeps on taking care itself. You keep on doing nothing and yet nothing is left undone. And you have confidence that will continue for as long as you live. Notice also, that your consciousness is changing but the consciousness of your cells remains unchanged. You do not have the power to change the consciousness of your cells.

Is it any wonder we can refer to our bodies as being wondrously magnificent?

But there is more to the story.

When you look deep into the human body with a microscope, you see that the cells are not attached to each other but have space around each cell. One could say that the human body is made up of more of that space than it is made up of cells because the space takes up more space than the cells do. What holds the cells together, to keep them in the shape of the human body? What holds those cells apart so that they do not touch each other? It is part of the knowingness that each cell has but it is a knowingness that we do not have in our minds.

We already know that we all have a wondrously magnificent human body. Now we get to the exciting part.

When one views a human cell one can see that each cell has sensors on it. What are the sensors for? What do the sensors do? Ask and you shall receive!

Those sensors are where sensations are placed when they are delivered to the body. The human body is where those sensations, or feelings, are experienced. Feelings are delivered to the sensors of our cells. Our cells know what to do when those feelings are delivered. Feelings are not delivered to all of our cells, just the right ones at the right time. For example, to create goose bumps on your arms, feelings are delivered to the cells of the arms to make that happen. In a similar way, feelings are delivered to the cells around the eyes to create tears of joy. Each time you feel good, that feeling was delivered to those cells that made you feel good.

God is everywhere. God is with me. God is with you. But did you know that God is also inside of your body? Did you know that God is not just in you a little bit but is inside each and every cell of your body? God is everywhere so there is nowhere that God cannot be. That includes the cells of your body. If God were not inside your body then God would not be everywhere and then God would not be God.

Any male or female on earth can go to any country on earth, meet with someone of the opposite sex, and have their respective ovum and sperm join together to start the process to create another human body. Males and females around the world are built to start this creation process.

But they don't create the new human; they simply place the sperm and ovum in proximity to get that process started. The creation begins when the sperm and ovum get together and create that first cell. That first cell knows what to do next and passes that knowingness on to all of the other cells it creates and each of them create. This continues until the entire body is created. God consciousness is in every human, no matter their nationality, ethnicity or race. Every human body on earth has this same God consciousness in it. Nothing about the wondrously magnificent human body needs to be changed to attain world peace. Actions of the body? Yes! But not the body itself.

You are not the all that God is but your body is full of part of God. God is love, joy, peace, harmony, unity, oneness and so much more. Your body is also therefore all of these. You are love but you are not the totality of the love that God is. You are joy but you are not the totality of the joy that God is. Likewise, for harmony, peace, unity and oneness. Your body is full of all of these. Your body cannot be emptied of these either. It is full of all of these and stays full of all of these all the time. To empty the body of these would be to remove God from your body and that you cannot do. With God in every part of your body you are therefore also full of love, joy, harmony, peace, unity and oneness.

God also knows all. God continues to know all, in each and every new moment. God did not just want to be in each of our bodies but

God had to be in each of our bodies. Here's why! As our body experiences an experience, our body knows that experience. It knows the feeling in that experience. It knows all of the senses and thoughts in that experience. In short, it knows that entire experience. Because God is in our body, God therefore also **knows** that experience as we **know** that experience. Without being **in** us, God would not know each experience as we know it and God would therefore no longer know all.

We had a wondrously magnificent body before we even knew how it was built to experience feelings. We had a wondrously magnificent body before we even thought about having God in every part of it. How do we find words to describe our wondrously magnificent bodies even better than that?

Man is God-made! You are God-made! God said that a knowingness that man is God-made is one of the important pieces needed for the creation of world peace. Not just a thought or belief but an actual knowingness that man is God-made.

God Is In You

You cannot love yourself without also loving God. You cannot love God without also loving yourself. As God is in you, so also is

God in every human being. Likewise, you cannot hate another person without also hating God, as a part of God is in that person you are hating. Because God is everywhere, God is in you and is in that person you are hating too. God is everywhere so God must also be in everyone.

Hurt yourself and you hurt your body and you hurt God, as God is experiencing that hurt as you experience it. God experiences that hurt as intimately as you experience that hurt. Smile and God experiences that smile as you experience it. Do something that makes you feel good and God feels good too. Give so much joy to another so that you cry tears of joy and God experiences your tears of joy too. Think of yourself as love, joy, harmony, peace, unity and oneness and God experiences you thinking that as well. You are happy. God is happy. I love it when I'm driving down the road and smile just so I can make God smile too. It's a powerful feeling and fun too. It's a great way to start the day, end the day, and improve all parts in between.

It's time for you to party! Celebrate your wondrously magnificent body! Celebrate every day. Celebrate every moment. We go to a party to enjoy the party, not to wait to the end of the party to enjoy only the end of it. Many live their lives expecting to party in the afterlife. Party also in the present life. Life is pre-sent, with gifts of experiences in every moment.

We go for a walk, not to get to the end of the walk but to enjoy the walk along the way in the present. We sit down to enjoy a great meal, not to get to the end of the meal but to enjoy the meal along the way in the present. Enjoy your journey.

Your wondrously magnificent body is yours to celebrate now. Treat your body as the temple it is, filled with God's love, joy, peace, harmony, unity and oneness.

All humans on earth, collectively, using all of the technology known to man, could not create one human body without the help of God. The fabulous, fantastic and awesome human body could only be created by God. Who but God could put these trillions of cells in exactly the right places, doing exactly the right things, at exactly the right time, and have them all working together harmoniously? Can you think of someone or something other than God who could create something as wondrously magnificent as the human body?

Connection with the divine is instinctual in humanity. That means you are connected to the divine, instinctually. It is your instinct to be. The impulse toward the divine is cellular. That means each of the trillions of cells in your body has an impulse toward the divine.

Now, therefore, since every one of your cells is instinctively connected to the divine and each has an impulse toward the divine, and each has that knowingness in it, you, as the whole of those cells, are also all of that.

From what little you understand of your body today, even in that understanding there is more God in you than there is you in you. You have a higher self and you are a higher self.

That change in consciousness we talked about earlier is occurring in you. Notice it! Appreciate it! Be grateful for it! Celebrate it! You are becoming an instrument of peace.

The energy of life is in the air and if you want more of the energy of life, breathe more! Fill your body with more of the energy of life and you are filling your life with more energy. Consciously direct the energy of life to your brain and you increase your awareness of life and your awareness of everything around you. You have expanded your consciousness. Once you experience the value of this exercise you may start experimenting with directing the energy of life to other parts of your body. Imagine the possibilities!

I strongly suggest you practice the following breathing exercise as often as possible.

Breathe

- o Breathe in.
- o Notice how you feel while taking in the energy of life.
- o Breathe deeply for a while
- o Picture this energy of life entering through an opening at the top of your head
- o Using your minds eye, watch as it moves through your body.
- o Breathe out
- o Let the energy exit through your feet.
- o Do this a number of times.
- o Next, picture filling your brain with this energy.
- o Feel the oxygen fill your brain, feeding and nourishing the cells there.
- o Do this intentionally for seven minutes.
- o Do not worry as you feel light-headed because you will be light-headed.
- o You have intentionally sent the golden white light of the energy of life to your brain.

- o This enlightens your brain cells and you may feel a sense of enlightenment.
- o With that physical feeling may come an increased awareness of life, of everything around you.
- o You have opened your mind, exposing it to the gentle breeze of expanded consciousness.

Now reread these steps!

I've used this breathing exercise many times and each time feels like a new experience. I think my trust in the process increases each time I use it and I believe, more each time, that I accept whatever is coming.

Breathing is the process by which the life force enters you, flows through you, and is sent by you back to life itself. Breathing is not something that you need to be told to do. You do it automatically because it is life serving. It is the first thing you do each moment.

Did you notice your consciousness change as you read this chapter? Stop and think, for a moment, how your thoughts have changed, from before reading this chapter, to now. Are you more conscious about how great your

body really is? And are you more conscious, now, about how great every human body is, how we should treat our body as a temple, and how we should treat every other body as a temple too? How can you or anyone be mean to a temple? Notice the consciousness shift you are going through on your path to becoming an instrument of world peace.

Once you get this,
once you truly get this,
you'll never go back
to what you were.

Your Soul

This chapter takes you through a consciousness shift concerning your soul. Notice how similar this sounds to the previous chapter description and yet how different this consciousness shift really is.

In the realm of understanding our soul, we are youngsters strutting around, saying things, doing things, but having little to no idea of our soul, its purpose, and its actions. These actions are actions we should be intimately aware of, knowledgeable about and adhering to. It would be for our own good and well-being.

It seems like a rather blurry statement when someone says or thinks that feelings are the language of the soul. Here is my understanding of what that means. When God created everything, one of the things God created was the Soul. God then set aside an individuated soul, a part of the Soul, for each and every one of us. That individuated part is **your soul** and yet it remains a part of **the Soul**. God did the same thing for every human being. Our individuated soul, that little part of the Soul, is the only constant in each of us. The body and the mind change but the soul does not. It is truth and does not change.

Our individuated soul, however, is not empty, like our mind is, when we start life in our new body. Our soul was created for us and not by us like our body is. It is the one constant in who and what we are.

Our individuated soul surrounds our body. You might picture it as many have drawn it, as an aura surrounding the body somewhat resembling the shape of the body. The center of our soul, the heart of our soul, also our second heart, is in our center. It is where our gut feelings originate. It is where our sixth sense or our sense of knowing resides.

Experiencing Our Life Plan

The individuated soul of a person holds the life plan of that person. My soul holds my life plan and your soul holds your life plan. My body and my mind do not know my life plan. It is only for the soul to know. Because your body and your mind do not know your life plan, your soul sends information to your body regarding your life plan.

Our life plan is the reason a new feeling is sent to our body in each and every new moment. In each new moment, the body is experiencing a new experience. The soul knows that experience right before it arrives and sends a feeling to make it part of, or a member of, that experience.

As it is experienced in the body, the body senses the feeling, and if we're paying attention, you notice the feeling. If it feels good, then you know that that experience is in alignment with your life plan. If that good feeling is missing, then you know that that experience is not in alignment.

The Creation Of ICURY.

I've created a special little character designed to help you better understand how the soul works. My name is ICURY. My job is to make very, very special deliveries to your body. I make my deliveries to your body every moment of your life. Your body notices each of my deliveries as I make them. When you pay close attention to all that your body is experiencing, you consciously notice each of my deliveries. What I deliver makes a difference in the quality of each of your moments and in the quality of your life.

I am not alone. I have lots of help. There are millions, even billions, of us making deliveries to your body. What we are delivering to your body is different than what we are delivering to every other body we deliver to. And yes, we deliver to every single human body.

Your body always notices when we make deliveries because we make millions of high impact deliveries to your body in an instant. We make our deliveries directly to the tiny cells of your body. We and what we are delivering are the reason you have many sensors on each of the cells of your body. Each of us place our delivery directly onto those sensors.

We may make our deliveries to different parts of your body but we always deliver to the sensors on the cells of your body. We make each of our deliveries super-fast. One could say we fly to make our deliveries. You might think of us as really tiny butterflies making deliveries to your body. Everyone loves us and what we deliver. Everyone loves butterflies like ICURY on the front cover.

We go to your soul to pick up our deliveries and from there deliver them to your body. The soul tells us what to deliver and where to deliver what we are delivering. Our deliveries are the way the soul communicates with or talks to your body. The soul knows the truth about your life plan and, at the point of our deliveries, the body experiences the truth about your life plan. The soul knows and the body experiences.

- Our mind thinks it knows based on what we have placed in our mind. Our soul knows based on what God has placed in our soul. Are you better served by acting on what you have placed in your mind or by what God has placed in your soul? Which do you think will serve you better? Pay attention to ICURY.

We deliver the soul's knowingness to the body using feelings. It is the way the soul speaks to the body and how the body hears the soul.

Our first deliveries started when your body started. Your soul and your body have been communicating every moment of your lives. This is the main communication between the body and the soul. Did you know this about your body and your soul? The body is wondrously magnificent! The soul is truth.

Because of our deliveries, every experience you have has a feeling as one of its members. An experience is never complete without a feeling.

Once we deliver a feeling to you, it is yours. It becomes yours simply by it being delivered to you and only you. It is your feeling in that moment, the moment you receive it.

You might ask, *"ICURY, why don't you deliver better feelings to me?"* Stop right there! I don't decide what I am delivering and I don't decide where I am delivering to. I simply deliver. It's what I do and I do it well. Your soul decides what I deliver to your body and your soul decides where in your body I deliver it to. Your soul knows. We simply deliver.

It's what the soul does. Your soul plays a major role in your life. How much you pay attention to your soul is up to you. You decide how much attention you pay to your soul. You can change your mind but you cannot change your soul.

Your Owned Feelings

By using your body and your mind, you are able to respond to feelings as they are delivered to you. A feeling that is delivered to you is **your** feeling. Yours! Only yours! You own it! You are responsible for your feeling. No one else is able to respond to your feeling. You are also not response able for someone else's feeling. Each feeling is personal, or body specific. It is yours and only yours.

Your soul plays a major role in your life, if you allow it to. Here again you are given free will to choose. You can receive feelings from your soul and choose to ignore them or you can receive feelings from your soul as directions to a path that will take you higher. Know that in both cases you are choosing. Know also that when you ignore your feelings you are living your life by chance whereas when you acknowledge your feelings and act accordingly, you are living your life by choice. By chance or by choice, you are choosing either way.

- Much study and research has been done to look deep inside the body to better understand it. Much study and research has also been done to look deep inside the mind to better understand it. It's time we looked deeper into our soul.

Every individual feeling your soul sends you is meant for you only. The feeling is yours and only yours. The feeling you receive has nothing to do with anyone else. It is a message about the path you are on and has nothing to do with anyone else's path. No one else can experience your feeling either. Everyone receives their very own feelings from their very own soul.

You also cannot experience their feelings. In your mind, you may think you know someone else's feeling. You can do this by having your mind recall how you felt in a similar situation. This is a reaction on your part. You are reacting the same way as when you first experienced your feeling. You therefore think you know someone else's feeling. You can't because their feeling is delivered by their soul and yours is recalled from your mind. Feelings recalled from the mind are feelings experienced earlier.

People want to feel like they have a purpose in life. When they find their soul, they find their purpose in life, their life plan. Then they will feel their purpose in life.

Our Soul Knows

Our soul is love, joy, unity, harmony, peace, oneness and much more. Our soul knows each of these and yet it is our soul's intention to know each of these experientially. Our soul cannot know each of these experientially in the soul alone. The soul can know in the soul but the soul cannot experience in the soul. The body does not know until it experiences and in that moment the soul also experiences. And then the soul also knows that experience which was the soul's intention all along. In harmony. In unity. In oneness.

When our body experiences love, our soul experiences that experience and thereby knows that experience. Our soul then knows love experientially which was our soul's intention all along.

Your soul is in you around you and in every cell of your body. Your soul cannot experience anything, by itself, so it must wait until you experience it in your body, at which time the soul also experiences it. Make your body happy and you make your soul happy.

Be Mindless

The soul understands what the mind cannot conceive. True celebration is mindless. In other words, celebrate with your body and soul while not thinking about it. The soul speaks to you in feelings. Listen to, follow and honor your feelings as they are your truth. When you act only out of what is true for you, you speed your way down the path. Get back to your senses. Thoughts are mental constructs, made up creations of your mind.

God says, *"The soul knows in its wisdom that the experience you are having in this moment is an experience sent to you by God before you had any conscious awareness of it. This is what is meant by a pre-sent experience. It's already on the way to you even as you are seeking it. For even before you ask, I shall have answered you."*

My Plan

I was born with a plan for my life. The plan knows why I am here. My plan knows what I am here to do, to accomplish, to learn, to become, to be. My soul knows my plan but does not talk to me in words about it. My soul uses feelings to communicate that plan to me.

My soul knows my life plan. My soul wants that part of me that is my body and my mind to know my soul plan too. First my soul sends a feeling. Next, my body senses the feeling as it becomes part of the current experience. Then my mind stores the experience which includes the feeling.

In addition, my soul wants to feel the feeling as it arrives in my body. To do that, the soul has placed itself inside of my body so it too can experience the feeling as it arrives. In this way, my soul gets to know my plan experientially. The soul is this plan.

My soul wants my plan brought to fruition through experiences I create. My soul sends me feelings. My soul is part of me. I, therefore, am sending me feelings. Those feelings become part of my experience and are stored in my mind. In this way I create my experiences.

By experiencing my plan my soul experiences itself. By experiencing what I am experiencing my soul is also experiencing God because God is in me and God and I are creating those experiences.

Why do you think the world has such strong feeling experiences going on? Pay attention. As people around the world have their feelings ignored, even by themselves because they are unaware, then there is an ever-growing need inside those people to genuinely feel good.

When they don't get it one place, they try another, even not knowing that they are searching for that better feeling. They blame others as that is what they learned to do from others, who also blame others, for their bad feelings. All the while everyone is going around trying to find that good feeling that someone else is keeping from them. Everyone is looking to someone else in an attempt to feel better. Too bad they don't know ICURY.

When we eat something that tastes good, we want to eat it again soon. Likewise, for sound, smell, etc. And yet, when we feel good, we often pay no attention to where those feelings are coming from. It's time we started noticing our good feelings and strive to repeat them as well. It would be for our own good and well-being.

Bringing Focus

Always, always, always, bring focus to the feeling of each experience, before the experience has passed. We have a history of giving focus to thoughts and actions and ignoring feelings. That provides us with a history of giving focus to mind and body and ignoring soul. Your soul is part of something bigger, the Soul. Your body is filled with something bigger, God.

As sure as you can prove that you have a soul you can also prove that you do not. Neither can be proven. At least they can't be proven either way when you involve only your mind. In other words, when you use only your thoughts to try to figure it out then you cannot get an honest answer. The answer you get by asking your mind is the answer that is already supported in your mind. However, when you add the body and the soul to the source of the answer, then you get the answer that is naturally you, not the normally you that you are used to getting by involving only your mind.

In a moment when you are making a great decision turn to your soul instead of to your mind. Your soul will help you make a great decision based on what God has placed in your soul. This will take you on a better path than if you used your mind to make the decision which would be based on what you placed into your mind.

Our soul is that most important part of who we are. We cannot touch our soul, hear our soul, see our soul, smell our soul or taste our soul. We cannot completely know our soul. Yet our soul plays a significant role in each and every experience we encounter.

To become one with God, our creator, one need only change one's mind. One need not, and cannot, change one's body or one's soul as they are already one with God. Your intention to become one with God would be much more of a task had you to also change your body or your soul to become one with God.

You are already a powerful attraction, of love, joy, harmony, peace, unity and oneness. Your soul attracts these naturally as that is what the soul is. It is in the very nature of the soul and you cannot change the nature of the soul. Your body also attracts these, naturally, as God is in your body.

You may attempt to convince yourself that God is not in you but that will only create a change in your mind and not in your body. And notice, really notice, that **you** created that change in your mind. You created the change, therefore you are a creator.

Finding Your Passion

Want to find your passion? It's easy! Pay attention to your feelings. The stronger the feeling, the closer you are to finding your passion. When I started to truly notice my feelings I started finding my passion. This book is the result of paying attention to my feelings. If reading this book feels good to you, notice that and know that your soul is also signaling your body that this is truth for you as well.

The more you act on your intuition, fearlessly, the more your intuition will serve you. Intuition is the ear of the soul and resides in the soul. Every feeling you've ever had resides in your soul. Your soul is the sum total of all your feelings. It is the repository. Your feeling preserve.

From what little you understand of your body today, even in that understanding there is more God in you than there is you in you. Now you also know that God is in your soul. You have a higher self and you are a higher self.

Some may seek to create balance of their soul, body and mind, such as the balance of a three-legged stool. To create balance is to create equal parts. The soul, body and mind are not equal and never will be. Seeking balance, therefore, can never be. Choose instead to create harmony, harmonious relations, within you, body, mind and soul. Your body, mind and soul are harmony. What is in your body is already in harmony with your soul and your mind. What is in your soul is already in harmony with your mind and your body. All that's left to do is for you to change what is in your mind so that it is in harmony with your body and your soul. The more love you place into your mind the more in harmony, with what your soul and your body already are you will be.

That change in consciousness we talked about earlier is occurring in you. Did you notice that change as you read this chapter? Stop and think, for a moment, how your thoughts, about your soul, changed, from before reading this chapter, to now. Are you more conscious of your soul and the role it plays in your life? Notice the consciousness shift you are going through on your path to being an instrument of world peace. Notice too, how you feel about that shift.

We've allowed our thoughts
to make us into who we are,
instead of learning who we are,
and making our thoughts
coincide with that.

Your Mind

This chapter takes you through a consciousness shift concerning your mind. Notice how different this consciousness shift is.

Do humans create their own thoughts or do thoughts come to humans from somewhere? Either way, a thought must be created before it can exist or come to you. To bring a thought into existence, do you create it or does God create it? What do you think? Where did the thought you just had about that come from?

Can you send that thought back? To where it came from? And if so, where is that?

Can you deny a thought you just had? Can you stop your next thought from coming?

I've just asked you nine questions. Now, quit thinking about that and think about this! Would it be normal for you to stop reading here and ask God for the answers to those questions? Or would it be normal for you to keep reading to get answers? Or would it be normal for you to determine your answers from what is already in your mind? Or would it be normal for you to look it up or ask someone else? What if it was in your nature to ask God but that was not what you normally do?

What is in your nature is what God built, or created. What is in your normal is what you built, or created. Which do you trust more? Which is likely closer to your truth? When your nature becomes your normal, how will you have changed your mind from what it is today?

Natural and normal are not the same thing. Normal means something usually done. Natural is how you are when you are not trying to be normal. In any given moment, you can do what you normally do, or you can do what comes naturally. Nothing is more natural than love. If you act lovingly, you will be acting naturally. If you react fearfully, resentfully, angrily, you may be acting normally, but you will never be acting naturally.

Thoughts are not feelings but rather, they are ideas of how you should feel. When thoughts and feelings get confused, truth becomes clouded and lost. To get back to your feelings, be out of your mind and get back to your senses. In other words, stop the thoughts coming from your mind by focusing your mind on your feelings instead. Once you know your truth, live it.

Perhaps it is time we give some thought regarding the source of what is entering our mind and who determines what is entering our mind.

A New Way Of Thinking

The main reason we will experience world peace soon is that we will all develop a new way of thinking. To which you'll likely think, *"What are you talking about?"* I can only imagine what I'd say if someone told me that I was going to learn a whole new way of thinking. Thinking is just something I do. There is no **way** of thinking. One just thinks or one just does not think. Or so I thought!

Can you predict what your next thought will be? You are always having a current thought but a current thought is a thought that has already been delivered to you. It is the one you are thinking about right now. What I am talking about here is that thought that follows that current thought you are having. What I am talking about is the thought you are going to receive next. The thought that is being put together for you and that you will receive next.

Can you decide what that next thought will be? If not, who decides that for you? Is someone or something else doing that? If so, who or what is deciding that? And why is that being decided for you?

How do you explain a thought that comes to you that is completely new to you? All of the thoughts that I wrote here were completely new to me at one time. Did they come from God or did I create them? I believe it is both.

Where does a thought come from when it is a thought that no other human being has ever had before? It might have resided in the mind since God created the mind. The words, or members, of the thought may have been attracted together to answer an earlier question you had. Who or what decided to put that thought together and who or what decided to send that thought to me?

It begs the question, "What is thinking?" This question needs to be answered before one can develop a better way of thinking to replace a current way of thinking.

What do you do to yourself to make yourself think? What we think about is often what we are talking or texting or writing about. People often think they know what we are thinking by what we are saying and or what we are doing. Have you given thought to how you think? Is your way of thinking the correct way of thinking? Is there a right way and a wrong way to think?

What is the mind? Do I have my very own mind or is my mind part of a larger mind, the mind of God? Exactly where is my mind?

Again, I asked and I received. When God created everything, one of the things God created was the Mind. The Mind is where all thoughts are stored, yours, mine and everyone's. When God created us, God took many small portions of the Mind and set one aside for each of us.

Individual minds are individuated parts of the Mind. My individuated portion is my mind and your individuated portion is yours. I have the use of my mind even while it remains a part of the Mind. We each have our own mind and we all share the Mind.

My brain converts my thoughts into a common energy language that is then stored in my mind. My thoughts can be in English, Spanish, German or any other language. All languages are converted to the same common energy language of the Mind for storage in our mind.

The Mind shares thoughts across minds. By having one energy language for the entire Mind, thoughts arriving are simply converted by the brain to the language that that brain knows. The Mind also allows members of an experience to separate from the experience, yet keeps track of them. In this way, a thought can be out on its own and can be fetched when someone does an "Ask and you shall receive."

I always thought I could recall thoughts because they were stored in my brain. I didn't know, then, that my brain converts my thoughts and stores them in my mind. It was quite mind changing.

Thoughts come to us as they are drawn in from the Mind. You draw thoughts to you through attraction. The you referred to here is the you that consists of your soul, your body and your mind.

Thoughts are drawn in by the pull, or attraction, of the mind, body and soul. A newborn has very little in its mind so most of the attraction comes from the body and soul. Since the body and soul are made up of, or filled with, love, joy, peace, unity, harmony and oneness, the thoughts the newborn has, or attracts, are primarily filled with love, joy, peace, harmony, unity and oneness. More of this is then attracted.

Over time, the newborn hears and learns things that start filling his/her mind with other than love, joy, peace, harmony, unity and oneness. More of that is then attracted.

Some hear and learn many things that are not love, joy, peace, harmony, unity and oneness and gradually the mind moves from attracting thoughts not filled with these.

Whenever you have bad thoughts followed by bad action, the bad that follows in your life is exactly what you ordered, because you are attracting that. You cannot blame anyone else for that, because you **cause** your own attraction, and no other body can do that for you or to you.

Out Of The Blue

Today we have so much information we need computers to help store it, search it, research it and make sense of it. Where did all of that information come from? Most of the information we get today is from someone else.

God says that when we say we receive information **out of the blue** we are right on, in that out of the blue is exactly where it is coming from. It is stored out there, in the air around us, beyond the air around us, in the blue. We see the blue sky where the information is coming from. It is where the mind is. It surrounds us.

One of the other things God created was thoughts. Thoughts are things and have energy. Thoughts needed to exist before thoughts could come to us. Thoughts needed to be stored someplace while they were waiting to come to us. God created the place to store those thoughts. We call this storage place the Mind.

When a thought comes to us **out of the blue**, it is coming from the Mind. That new thought becomes a member of the present experience in which it was received. That **experience** is then stored in the mind.

Brilliant ideas come to us in this way. Our desires have energy and when we place enough energy into our experiences we start attracting like energy to us. In many cases, a brilliant new idea is received by someone who is asking and receiving. When a person receives a brilliant new idea, that person becomes excited, happy, etc. This normally results in an experience with feelings closer to love than to fear. Those experiences therefore attract more experiences of love.

Receiving thoughts **out of the blue** is receiving thoughts from the Mind, thoughts that God put there when God created thoughts. But God did not create all thoughts when God created the Mind. God left room for mankind to create more thoughts. As man creates more thoughts and does so with God inside every cell of the body, man is co-creating those thoughts with God. It is therefore, even after this co-creation, correct to say that God created everything. It is also correct to say that man is also creating. God is co-creating with man. Man is co-creating with God. God is experiencing creation through man which is why God created man in the first place.

Feeling Good

It is part of your nature to desire to feel good. As you receive a feeling, that feeling is in response to a thought you are having. That feeling is a signal concerning that thought. If the feeling you receive is not a good feeling, know that you can change your thought and that requests a new feeling. If that new feeling is not a good feeling, choose again. Keep this up until you receive a good feeling. In this way, you will know you are on a path that is in alignment with your plan.

For example, let's say you are very angry at someone and you have a thought that you should 'smack that person'. As you have that thought, notice that the feeling that arrived with it does not feel good. You choose again. You choose a new thought to simply 'yell at that person' instead. The feeling that arrives now does not feel good either. So, you choose to just 'smile'. The feeling that arrives with the smile feels good.

You accept the good feeling and move on to your next experience. Your good feeling experience has now been stored in your mind and starts to attract similar experiences.

You are now living your life by choice and not by chance. You are living your life consciously. You have just completed a change in your consciousness. You consciously chose to keep changing your thought until the thought was accompanied by a good feeling. You consciously caused that experience to contain a member of love, your smile, before that experience was stored in your mind.

You are living consciously. You are conscious of the feeling you are experiencing, then rejecting it by choosing a new thought, until the feeling is one you choose to accept, and move on. If it does not feel good, think again! You are developing a whole new way of thinking.

Feelings are simple. There is no guesswork with feelings. Feelings never lie. You can always trust them. At times, you can feel it in your gut and you can always trust your gut.

Our Path

Our feelings move us or drive us along one path or another. Our thoughts choose which path we are driving on. By paying attention to our feelings, we can drive ourselves to a better life. Do you desire a better life? All desires are held with the belief that they will feel better once those desires are achieved. A better life would be here if we all simply changed the way we process thought in every moment of our lives.

The mind is so very much more than just storage space. It is the all that the Mind is, in harmony, unity and oneness of the all.

Some will find it hard to believe that thoughts come to us from out of the blue. Some may say that can't be or we would have known about it before. Scientists would have found that out by now. We'd see them if that was true! Yet, we know oxygen comes from out of the blue, in the air we breathe. We also know we create carbon dioxide in our bodies and breathe that out into the blue. Do we see either of them? Can we not see them and yet believe they are there? Oxygen feeds our bodies. Carbon dioxide feeds our trees and plants.

The surface area of my lungs, if spread out on the ground, would cover a complete tennis court. Breathe in. Do you feel the oxygen being taken out of the air by your lungs? Breathe out. Do you feel the carbon dioxide being placed in the air you breathe out? Do you tell your lungs to take the oxygen out of the air or place the carbon dioxide into the air? No! The body knows to do all that.

So too with asking questions and receiving answers. We do not need to know all of the details of the process in order to believe the process occurs. (But feel free to ask those questions of God if you want answers for that.)

Just as our body knows how to take a part of each breath and deliver that part of oxygen to a certain place in the body, so does the body know what to do with an answer that has been delivered to your brain. You already have lots of proof of this happening. Think about the times you tried to figure something out. What is the act of 'figuring something out' if not asking and receiving? Someone asks you a question. You place the question into your mind. You know the answer. What is this if not asking and receiving? By hearing the question, it is automatically placed into your mind. You don't immediately know the answer. There is more discussion. The answer comes to you. What is this if not ask and you shall receive?

This is not something new you need to learn to do. It is a part of you because you've been doing it all your life. Now that you've figured this out, you have free will to keep asking other people the questions or you can change to asking the questions of God. Which do you think will better serve you moving forward? Which is more likely to give you the truth? Which do you think will feel better?

All that is in one's mind is the result of what one has chosen to put there. Free will allows us to choose. No one can do that for us or to us. We are each response able to change our mind by what we choose to put into our minds. We are each responsible for what we have placed in our mind. Every single thing in my mind is there after having gone through my free will choosing before putting it there.

Storing Experiences

Another really interesting thing about our mind is that it does so much more than just store our thoughts. Our mind stores our thoughts and also stores our experiences.

Each experience consists of what we will call members of that experience. Members of an experience include but are not limited to;
- o feelings
- o bodily reactions to the feelings (ie. goosebumps)
- o thoughts
- o bodily reactions to the thoughts (ie. smile)
- o sensory information(sounds, tastes, smells, etc)
- o and things not yet known

With each experience we experience, our brain is busy converting the members of the experience into energy that our mind can work with. It's vitally important that every bit of energy in our mind works harmoniously with all the energy already in our mind. That energy must work harmoniously in our mind as well as in the Mind. The individuated mind and the brain are one, but not the same. They operate in harmony, unity and oneness.

Think of our mind as being full of radio waves. We can't see or feel radio waves but they are all around us. Devices have been built to create and send radio waves and other devices have been created to receive radio waves. Radio waves can even travel in and through us and we don't notice them doing that. Radio waves are energy in a form we cannot see, touch, hear, smell or taste. Yet when a radio receives the radio waves, it converts it into sounds we can hear. With radio waves, mankind emulated nature.

Thoughts, feelings and experiences are all stored in different ways. Energies stored in our mind can have vastly different wave lengths, oscillations, vibrations as well as other energy attributes. For example, feelings color thoughts and experiences. Look at a rainbow and you get a glimpse of a myriad of feelings stored in the Mind. A rainbow is beautiful as the Mind is beautiful!

You do not have control over **whether** an experience is placed into your mind or not. Each and every experience is placed into your mind whether you like it or not. The only control you have is over **what** each experience contains **before** it is placed into your mind. During that occurrence, you have a short period of time in which you can alter what that experience contains. Once experienced, all experiences are stored in the mind.

Attracting

As you place experiences into your mind they immediately start attracting similar experiences. In other words, they start attracting experiences of similar energy. The stronger the energy of the experience the stronger the energy of the attraction.

So what gives one experience more power than another? Love! Here is how that works. While you are experiencing an experience, you have free will to add love to that experience, or not to add love. Add a feeling of love to the experience and that experience, while stored in the mind, will attract similar experiences of love to you.

The feeling stored with the experience determines the attraction power of that experience. Add an experience to your mind that is absent the feeling of love and that experience will have a lower power of attraction in the mind. It will still attract but not at the power that love does. Your free will allows you to choose how much attraction power you want to give to each experience you store.

Attraction between experiences is more heavily swayed by the energy of each experience. An experience such as squeezing your finger will attract other experiences of squeezing your finger. If you, however, squeeze your finger and instantly become angry, that experience is stored with anger. You are now attracting more experiences that have anger as a member.

When you squeeze your finger again, and become angry, but instantly replace the anger with love, that experience is stored with love. Love is now a member of that new experience and is attracting more love.

Love has far more attraction power than anger. The anger experience will be overpowered by the love experience. You are better than you were before and you will now keep attracting more experiences with love as a member.

In this example, you now have two experiences of squeezing your finger stored in your mind. One has anger as a member and one has love as a member. Since love has far more attraction power, in the mind, than anger, you will be attracting more experiences with love as a member into your life. You will feel better.

You can take this a step further. We call it remembering. God calls it re-member-ing. Stop and think for a moment about squeezing your finger and having anger with that experience. With each thought about that, you are asking your mind to go fetch that experience which is stored in your mind.

You'll likely remember it. Your mind will likely fetch it for you. Then you receive it. You asked and you received. Now the memory of that experience is fresh in your mind. You are re-experiencing that experience of squeezing your finger the first time. You are reliving that experience. Now, with that experience in mind, simply decide to replace the anger in that experience with love. Consciously think about replacing the anger you remember and place love in its place.

In this moment, you will have a newly created experience, this time with love as a member, and this newly experienced experience gets stored with love instead of with anger. Then you move on to your next experience. You would now have three experiences of squeezing your finger in your mind, but now there will be two with love and one with anger.

You're winning. You're feeling better. You are better. You are better than you were before. All you had to do was change your thinking, your beliefs and your mind to live a better life. You didn't even have to squeeze your finger a third time to make the change in your mind.

You Create Experiences

You create every experience that you have. You provide the members of each experience. Your body through its six senses provides those members of an experience. Your mind provides the thought member of an experience. Your soul sends a feeling to your body where your body experiences that feeling which then provides the feeling member of an experience. You also provide the action or actions member of an experience. You create each experience you ever have. God said, *"I created you so I could enjoy you experiencing creating."*

Ask And Receive

Have you ever talked directly to your God? Your Jehovah? Your Allah? Your concept of God? Do you ask? Do you receive? Do you believe you can ask and also receive?

What is praying if not asking? If you've asked and not received, did you quit asking? Did you ask and expect to receive? Did you ask and then expect to receive an answer immediately? Did you ask and expect an answer, on your schedule? What if the answer came later when you weren't paying attention? What if the answer came in a different form than just words out of the blue? Would you notice? Would you consider it an answer to your question if it came in a form other than words?

Consider all of the information in your mind right now. Where did it come from? Is any of that information directly from God? If not, why not? If it is not directly from God, then it is filtered! Most people have filled their minds with what others have told them. Information received from others is filtered through those people's minds. It may be true or it may not be true. It may be right for them but not right for you.

The information they gave to you that you placed into your mind was filtered by that other person before you received it. Even if they received it directly from God, it went through their mind before they passed it on to you. The person you heard it from could have received it from somewhere or somebody where it was also filtered. How many layers of filtering has the information you have in your mind been through? Getting information directly from God results in that information arriving for you unfiltered. It is pure. You can trust it.

Everything in this book is filtered. At a minimum, it is filtered through my mind. Some is filtered through numerous people's minds. Even the information I received directly from God and wrote in this book is filtered. What you are reading are words that I took from my mind and put into this book.

How much of the information that you have in your mind is helping you today? Is it helping you to be better than you were before? Is it serving you on your life path?

When someone tells you something and you're not sure if it is true, why do you ask someone else? Why not ask God?

It's amazing that we were taught to get answers from experts, teachers, parents, grandparents, clergy and others but were not raised to get answers from God. It's amazing that we were taught to trust experts, teachers, parents, grandparents, clergy and the like but not raised that we could trust answers from God.

Are you happy? Chances are you've been happy many times in your life. Once you experience happiness you know what that is when it comes along again. You often do things that make you happy because you like being happy. If you did not like being happy, then you would not do things to be happy again. You like being happy because it makes you feel good and you like to feel good. Now do you know why?

Dad often said 'figure it out' when I asked him questions he did not have answers to. It made me so damn mad when he said that because I thought I deserved an answer. I was too young to figure it out, or I just didn't want to figure it out. Little did I know at the time that by living a life wherein I was constantly 'figuring it out', I would continue to try to figure things out all my life, including figuring out life. I always had questions about things well after others had gone on to other things. Thanks, Dad, for laying that foundation.

You Cause God's Feelings

You are living with God in you, everywhere inside you. God is living with you, inside and outside of you. You are living together.

Think about how you feel when you do something and experience a bad feeling. Now think about how you feel when you do something and experience a bad feeling, knowing that you are causing God to experience that bad feeling too? What did ICURY deliver to you with that thought?

Consciously consider what you are doing to yourself when you allow yourself to experience a bad feeling. Having bad feelings has been a normal part of your life. That is, before you knew how to stop having bad feelings. That is, of course, only if you choose to stop having them.

A feeling is not something you have as you have fingers and you have a face, legs, arms, eyes, and so on. It is not something you can own. It is not yours to have. Rather, a feeling is something you experience. The experience of a feeling is something you do have. It is also something only you can have. The experience is yours and only yours.

You experience a feeling in a moment and then you move on to the next moment where you experience yet another feeling. This is true for every moment of your life. Each of those feelings is a new creation and each of those experiences is also a new creation.

The feeling you notice in this moment may feel similar to the feeling of the previous moment. You may even think it is the same feeling. But thinking that does not make it so. The feelings are separate, individual, feelings, each a new creation, sent by your soul, one per experience.

Think of what happens when you create a visual in your mind's eye. You have a visual of what it is you are creating. It is not yet a solid or material thing. It is a picture in your mind of what you are now in the process of creating. Just as that 'thing' can exist in the mind's eye, so too can God exist inside every thing. All that's needed for you is to place God in your mind so it is true there too just as it always has been before, in your body and soul.

Think By Chance Or By Choice

I said earlier that you would learn a new way of thinking by reading this book. Here is a description of your old way of thinking, by chance and your new way of thinking by choice.

The process of chance: (Your old way of thinking.)

- You have a thought.
- You have a feeling about that thought.
- You **disregard** the feeling.
- You act on the thought.
- Your experience is stored in the mind.
- Your stored experience attracts similar experiences.

The process of choice: (Your new way of thinking.)

- You have a thought.
- You have a feeling about that thought.
- You **notice** the feeling.
- The feeling is good. You go to the next step

- The feeling is not good. You consciously choose a new thought and repeat this process.
- You act on the thought and feeling.
- Your experience is stored in the mind.
- Your stored experience attracts similar experiences.

Notice that both of these steps contain feelings, thoughts and actions. The **choice** process is how you were created to notice your feelings and act **naturally**. The **chance** process is what you have created to ignore your feelings and act **normally**.

The choice process is your new way of thinking provided, of course, that you have chosen to notice your feelings. You may find it easier to stay with your old way of thinking. You have free will to make that choice as well. Know that your choice is your ability to respond or your response ability in action. No one else has responsibility to your noticing your feelings or not noticing your feelings. It is your responsibility and only yours.

Your previous actions may have been normal for you but they may also have been unnatural for you. Following the choice process steps will move you from what you did normally to what you do naturally. This process will align you with your very nature.

You will start living your life by choice instead of by chance.

Everything that happens to you is caused by what you think in your mind and what you believe in your heart.

When you think lots of good thoughts your mind fills with good thoughts. Then your mind attracts even more good thoughts. You feel good. This attracts even more good feelings. Your life becomes better. Your life fills with goodness. You become good energy. You are good energy. You attract more good energy.

Our beliefs about ourselves come from our thoughts about ourselves. If I was in a car accident and lost all of my memory, I would no longer have any thoughts or beliefs in my mind about who I was. So, before the accident I could think things about myself such as, I'm bad, I'm mean, I'm dumb, I'm ugly, and so forth. After the accident, I wouldn't think or believe any of those thoughts. Yet, I'd be the same person.

We certainly don't need car accidents to change our minds. We've allowed our thoughts to make us into who we are, instead of learning who we are, and making our thoughts coincide with that.

Stress is something our mind gives to our body. It is also only our mind that can remove it. To put stress on the body is to put force, pressure or strain upon it. Change the stress by changing the mind. For example, I put the thought into my mind that I will be late for work and could get fired. This fear puts stress on my body. Or I put the thought in my mind that I'll be on time and have a great day. No fear and no stress. Either way I'll arrive at the same time.

Confidence does not come naturally to many people. Even the most successful people have struggled with it in their careers. You can develop confidence, just like any muscle or character trait, if you're willing to work at it. Step out of your comfort zone. Don't compare yourself with others. Compare yourself to what you were before. Ask yourself, "Am I better than I was before?" You, and only you, are in charge of that. Decide to be better than you were before. Your confidence will grow naturally.

People who depend on thoughts, absent noticed feelings, will move slowly on the path to world peace. People who depend on thoughts and the good feelings surrounding those thoughts will move quickly on the path to world peace. Get a move on.

Looking back on my life, how would it have changed had I gone from just thinking to consciously creating my thoughts on purpose and did that with the idea in mind that I was creating a future more closely aligned with the path of my soul?

We heard for years that all people want peace of mind. What is peace of mind? To create peace of mind, place more thoughts of peace into your mind. Fill your mind with thoughts of peace and you will affect peace in your mind. Do this with thoughts of love, joy, harmony, unity and oneness as these words are all interchangeable with peace. Your mind will become full of peace.

Creating Thought

When we have a thought, we create that thought. We do that by taking thought that is in the Mind and bringing those pieces or members together to create our very own thought. We add to what we receive from the Mind and create a new thought which then gets added to our mind. As God says, it must be so.

To have a thought exactly like someone else's thought would result in duplication. There is not duplication, only creation. Every single one of our thoughts is a new creation. Every thought we have is a thought we created. We've been creators all of our lives. Now we're moving from being unconscious creators to being conscious creators. Another change in consciousness is occurring in you. Be grateful it's that easy to create a new way of thinking.

We become the creators of our own thoughts by 'calling together' parts of those thoughts, from the Mind to our mind. God calls that re-member-ing. The members of a thought are the words included, or 'called together or asked together', to create that thought, or more accurately, re-create that thought.

New experiences are created every moment. God is doing that and we are doing that. God gets to experience our creations by being part of us, by being in us. We get to experience creation by God being in each of us as we create. God gets to experience my creations as I create them and God gets to experience your creations as you create them, but you and I do not get to experience each other's experiences. Nobody gets to experience any other person's experiences.

Create thought deliberately. You also create what you desire in your life. However, if you are more aware of what you do not desire, then what you desire cannot be manifested. You control whatever it is you manifest into your life. Be conscious of which you are more aware of.

You have thought accompanied by a strong desire and a strong feeling. Immediately upon entering the Mind it begins to attract. The attraction process continues. Repeating this sends a second thought that also attracts. Each one you send causes more attraction. You will soon be receiving. You must then allow.

Having some of those thoughts and then a thought of doubt starts a different, new attraction, of doubt, the opposite of the first thought. For example, I have a thought that I desire that many people buy this book. This starts attracting buyers. But I follow that thought with the thought that money is bad which I heard from my parents many times. This thought creates doubt and overrides my desire. Paying attention to your feelings allows you to know if you are giving your attention to your desire or if you are giving it to doubt, the absence of your desire. You can have thought or the absence of thought in an experience. You can have feeling but never the absence of feeling in an experience. The feeling is either good or the absence of good but there is always a feeling.

This is always going on in you, but when you consciously align with your feelings, your creative endeavors become so much more satisfying. The degree to which you feel blessed and expect good things to flow to you indicates the level of your state of allowing. Your feelings are your guidance system. Repeat a thought often enough and it becomes a belief. A belief has strong feelings attached.

We would have been well served, as children, had we been taught to weigh each thought and the feeling associated with it.

We dealt earlier with re-member-ing who we are. We brought the soul back in as a member of the all that we are, our body, mind and soul. The soul was there when we were babies, and between then and now we ignored it. Bringing the soul back into our consciousness now allows for the inclusion of feeling in our consciousness. Bringing feeling back into our moment by moment consciousness allows us to re-member our experiences. That is, if we choose to do so.

Imagine a thought that has a feeling of shame associated with it; then consciously create a new instance of that thought with a feeling of joy. The feeling of joy has replaced the feeling of shame in that experience. You chose to make that change.

For example, as a boy I created a thought with a feeling of shame associated with it. It was one of my crowd(the people I listened to) thoughts. It wasn't until now that I took that thought and re-member-ed it with a feeling of joy. This I did by adding a knowingness, which includes that everything happens for a reason, and that reason was that I got to have that experience so that I could be exactly where I am today. Where I am today is in perfect plan with what my soul chose for me to be.

As I started reexamining my beliefs, and noticing my feelings about each belief, only then could I consciously keep or discard that belief and allow it into the present, and therefore into my future.

You, A Creator

Think about something you invented. What have you built that is different than anything you know of? When you place words together into a sentence, do you think of that sentence as an invention? At one point, that sentence was the first time you re-member-ed those words into that sentence for you, by you. You created that sentence. Since words are energy and sentences are energy, then you manipulated energy. Since everything is energy, you can create using energy to make other energy.

You can invent. You can build. You can create. You are a creator.

Did you ever think you were creating when you spoke a sentence? Notice how your consciousness change is occurring. It's that easy and painless.

As a young man I did not know that some of my thoughts were hurting me. I also did not know that some of my thoughts were helping me. I did not know I could choose to consciously create my thoughts so that they would all help me. I did not know I could consciously piece my thoughts together in such a fashion that they coincide with my goals, my desires, my plans.

I did not know I could create thought. I did not realize I was creating by my creating experiences in every moment. I thought things just happened to me. I did not know I could create a happening. I did not know I was creating each experience or happening as I was experiencing it. I also did not know that in all cases I did create all of my experiences.

An idea comes to you out of the blue. You were not thinking about it at all. Your thoughts were on something completely different. This is how the universe delivers what we ask for. Some time, before now, you were thinking about something related to the idea. You got sidetracked and quit thinking about the idea.

But before you did, you requested more info about the idea. Maybe it was something as simple as saying 'I wonder . . . . about this idea'. You may have had the same idea come to you quicker if you would have become silent right after wondering. We cannot force a thought to form a completely new thought or idea. We can only attract. And we attract by defining and stating clearly and then by allowing.

Allowing means listening. It may be difficult for you to listen. It may be even more difficult to listen and at the same time clear your mind of all thought. One way to do that is to place yourself in a peaceful spot. Then relax and start breathing deeply. Concentrate on each breath in and each breath out. Once you have achieved concentration, listen to the sounds of your breath.

Trust in the value of your insight. When you are given an idea or thought or invention, treat it as very important. It is! Everything happens for a reason. The reason you were given the idea, thought or invention is because it is an answer to your request and it coincides with your soul plan.

Treat all your thoughts as important. Do the same when you get an intuitive flash! When a thought leaps into your mind! When you get an intuitive feeling that something is right! When that small voice within speaks to you! Listen! Listen to your gut! Your gut will speak to you, in the language of the soul with feeling.

You can think you know something but until you sense that you know for sure, you do not feel that you know. Without doubt! See a bumblebee fly. It knows it can fly. And scientists can prove the bumblebee cannot fly. The earth is round. We know it is round. And yet, for centuries, the human race believed that it was flat. For centuries humans also believed the earth was the center of the universe. Now we know that the sun is the center of our solar system and our solar system is just a tiny speck in the universe.

For centuries humans knew that humans couldn't fly and yet today millions of humans fly every day. Today our knowingness has changed to know we can fly. Notice how our knowingness has changed over the years and yet the truth has not. Our soul and the feelings it sends us are truth, always. Our minds and what is in them is not always truth. Too often we have been satisfied with information that is too far removed from the source. Ask and you shall receive from the source.

Know your higher self. This is the self that is mind, body and soul. You do not have to create God as that has been done. You need only allow God into your mind. God is already in your soul and in your body. Let God into your mind and you will know your higher self.

Changing your mind is simply choosing again. In most cases, we do it without conscious thought about changing our minds. In order for you to change your mind you must already have something in your mind to change from. You know you cannot choose when there is only one thing to select.

For example, you cannot choose love if love is the only thing to choose from. You can choose love when you have both anger and love to choose from. You can also choose anger if you so choose. When you choose, which do you choose? Do you realize you are choosing in every single moment of your life? How have the choices you have made in your life, so far, served you?

The process goes something like this. You gather enough information into your mind to convince you that what you know is true. Others believe it too. You have the evidence. You do this often enough and long enough and you know it for sure, without a doubt. This becomes your truth.

Notice that I said, "becomes" your truth. In the act of becoming, it experiences change in order to become what it becomes. Truth does not change, ever. Therefore, your thoughts cannot become truth. They are or they aren't truth - nothing more, nothing less.

Truth was truth before you started thinking about it. Can you simply think about something long enough to make it a truth, or is a truth a truth before you start thinking about it? Can you think about something that is an untruth and eventually make it a truth? Likewise, can you think about something that is a truth and eventually make it an untruth?

When I say "I know!", who and what am I speaking for? I am made up of three parts, my mind, my body and my soul. When I say, "I know!" am I speaking for my body and my soul or just for my mind? Can I know anything, for sure, without including my soul which is my truth?

This book is filled with my truth. You are reading my truth. How will you know which parts are true for you? Very simply! As you read, notice your feelings about what you are reading.

Everything in this book came from my mind. Everything in this book came from the Mind. Some things in this book came from the minds of others. All three of these statements are true. Here's how that can be? Thought originated when the creator created thought and placed it in the Mind. All humans receive thought into their individuated minds from the Mind through attraction. Humans also receive thoughts from other humans.

In order for me to write this entire book, I needed at some point to have all of the thoughts in this book in my mind. This holds true whether I received the thoughts from others or directly from the Mind. As with everything, there is also oneness in and with the Mind.

Trillions of super tiny particles, called neutrinos, zip through our bodies every second. We do not see or feel them but we know they are there. They are similar to radio waves and they come from the sun and stars and come from all directions.

They do not collide and explode. They get along harmoniously. They zip through space at close to the speed of light. Scientists claim that about 60 billion solar neutrinos pass through our thumb nails every second. Just as we cannot see those trillions of neutrinos, so too we cannot see the mind or its contents, out in the blue. Scientists claim the neutrinos exist as described here. God says the mind exists as described here. Which do you trust as your truth? If you don't believe what is written here, simply ask and you shall also receive your answer.

A life lived by choice is a life of conscious action. A life lived by chance is a life of unconscious reaction. Re-action is just that, an action you have taken before. When you react, you search your memory bank for the same or nearly the same experience and act the way you did before. This is all the work of the mind and not of the soul.

Be aware of and control your thoughts as you pray. Think only good thoughts absent negativity and darkness. Especially in moments when things look bleak express gratitude and joy will come your way.

Your world will follow your idea about yourself. You have no choice in this matter as it is the only matter in which you have no free choice. It is simply the way it is. First you'll have the thought about yourself that you are mind, body and soul and this will lead to the outer world of physical manifestation.

What you	**think**	you	create
What you	create	you	become
What you	become	you	express
What you	express	you	experience
What you	experience	you	are
What you	are	you	**think**

The circle is complete and you have caused yourself to know this. You have also caused yourself to care more than ever before who you really are, mind, body and soul.

That change of consciousness that we talked about earlier continues to occur. We are moving closer to world peace, one being at a time.

If a newborn baby was taken from a family with a certain religious belief and that baby was secretly exchanged with a newborn baby from a family with a competing religious belief, both babies would be raised with competing beliefs and those beliefs would become their own.

The babies, now adults, would only know their beliefs, and would not know they should have the competing beliefs. Eventually these adults are fighting each other, each not knowing they are on the opposite side of what they were born to be raised as. Logic would dictate that since both of them are on the wrong side there is no right side. And if there is no right side then there cannot be a wrong side. Or can they both be right and both be wrong? And what about them would be right or wrong? As you can see from this example, the difference between the right and the wrong is only the beliefs. In other words, they are only right or wrong depending on what they have in their minds.

They have each individually placed into their minds everything that is in their minds. Observe the condition and circumstances of the world today and then give thought to what part the human mind contributes to that condition and those circumstances.

While thinking of something, give a little thought to what the opposite is. If you find you are also thinking in the area of the opposite, then you consciously know that you are thinking the opposite of what you want to be thinking. At this point deliberately focus on the positive and only the positive of that something.

Love is a very high vibrational offering. Fear is a very low vibrational offering. Once you understand your emotions and the important messages they are giving you, you will not have to wait until something has manifested in your experience to understand what your vibrational offering has been – you can tell, by the way you feel, exactly where you are headed.

You have thoughts of a new idea. The energy of attraction works on your **most recent** thoughts of that idea. The energy of attraction works better when you have **frequent** thoughts of that idea. It works even better when you **focus** on those frequent thoughts of that idea. And it's even better yet when you **add emotion** or feeling energy to your thoughts of that idea.

Consciously make the energy of attraction work for you. Because the energy of attraction works on your **most recent** thoughts, make your new thoughts, as many as possible, thoughts of love, joy, peace, unity and you will be attracting more of each of them.

Do you want peace? If so, ask for it. Be careful of the wording of your request. For example, do not say you **want** peace. By saying you want peace you announce that you do not have peace. If you do not have peace you **cannot give** peace. If you do not have peace, then you cannot attract peace. If you desire peace, thank God for peace, **gift peace** to another, and you will know you have peace or you could not have given it to another. Gift peace and you will attract even more peace.

In the moment you choose peace, in that moment human beings are instantly more peace full. Thank God. When gratitude replaces judgment, peace spreads throughout your body, gentleness embraces your soul, and wisdom fills your mind.

Happiness is a state of mind. With all states of mind, it produces itself in physical form. All states of mind reproduce themselves.

Peace is a state of mind. Think about it! Deciding ahead of time what you choose to be will produce that in your experience. Decide to be peace and you will produce peace in your experience.

Every thought you have is either sponsored by fear or it is sponsored by love. Although a thought could be sponsored by a derivative of one of these it ultimately breaks down to one of these. In the end there is only love. When fear is used effectively it is an outgrowth of and expresses love. A parent saving a child from a burning house is love expressed as fear. God is absolute love.

Love and fear are natural emotions. We are born with two fears, the fear of falling and the fear of loud noises. The reason we are born with these two fears is simply to build in a bit of caution. All other fears are learned responses. We were taught these fears by our parents or learned them from our environment.

Love and fear are tools given to you at birth to help you along your path in life. These natural emotions, when repressed as they are in most people, result in unnatural reactions and responses. Both emotions, when used as the gifts they are, assist you on your life path.

Decide ahead of time to be love or to be fear. Your choice will be produced in your experience. Your choice is that powerful. It's that simple.

Imagine a life without love. A baby without love soon dies.

Imagine a life without fear. Peace, joy, love, harmony, unity and oneness would guide you on a blissful soul path journey.

Today's normal human brings fear into their lives in many ways not even aware that they are making that choice. Notice the fear used on you while you watch or listen to the news. Fear of terrorists, evildoers, lawbreakers and much more. Notice the fear used on you as you attend a religious service. Fear of punishment, burning in hell, outcast and much more. Other fears you bring on yourself such as fear of being late for work, not making payments on time, someone becoming angry at what you said or something you did. Notice where else you experience fear. Remove yourself from it. Choose to experience love instead. Do this by deciding ahead of time to be love and you will produce love in your experience.

In human relationships be concerned only for yourself. Make the highest choice for the self. In oneness, this becomes the highest choice for another. The highest choice for one is the highest choice for all.

For example, I could want my life partner to be love. This is a mistake in that I should instead be love myself as that is a far higher choice than to attempt to choose for another. I cannot know what is best for my life partner who is on her soul path. Only she can do that. I can however know what is best for me on my soul path. Choose for self only and allow others their own choices.

Each choice is self-creative. Each choice defines you. Each choice gifts God seeking to know himself experientially. God is God in the act of creating himself. So too am I. My soul longs to do so too. This is that for which my spirit hungers.

That change in consciousness we talked about earlier is occurring even more than before. Are you noticing? What about your mind, as you understood your mind before, changed as you read this chapter? Do those changes feel good? These consciousness shifts are propelling you on your path to being an instrument of world peace. Notice who you are 'being', now, and how that has shifted from who you were 'being' before.

Experiences

This chapter takes you through a consciousness shift about experiences. You will learn how you are creating each of them, how you can choose and change each of them into experiences that will better serve you. You will begin to understand how you can consciously improve every moment so that you will move faster on your path to experiencing world peace.

An experience is not something that just happens to you. You create it! How many of the experiences you've had in your life would you have changed to better experiences had you known you could do that?

The purpose of each experience is to create opportunity. Events and experiences are opportunities. Nothing more, nothing less. They are things that happen. It is what we think of them, do about them, respond to them, that gives them meaning.

Events and experiences are opportunities drawn to you, created by you individually or collectively, through consciousness. Consciousness creates experience. You are attempting to raise your consciousness to become the higher self that you now know you are being. You have drawn these opportunities to you in order that you might use them as tools in the creation and experiencing of who you are. You are a being of higher consciousness than you are now exhibiting.

The soul knows in its wisdom that the experience you are having in this moment is an experience sent to you by God before you had any conscious awareness of it. That is what is meant by pre-sent experience. It's on its way even as you are seeking it, for even before you ask, God shall have answered you. Every now moment is a glorious gift from God. That's why it is called the present.

It is the soul's desire to bring you back to God. It is the soul's intention to know itself experientially, and thus to know God. For the soul to know itself experientially, the soul must be in your body where experiencing is done. For the soul understands you and God are one, even as the mind denies this truth and the body acts out this denial.

Imagine, for a second, that God mixed things up and created you as the Soul instead of creating you as the you that you now are. So, in this imagining, you are now the Soul. You are truth and you know the life plan of every human. Your desire is to know yourself experientially. But, as the Soul, you do not have a human body to experience experiences in, nor will you ever have a human body. All knowing, you know that the human body can experience happenings and you know that it does so in every moment. So, then, you and God get together and take a little part of you, the Soul, and designate it for me, or for my use only. You call that little part of the Soul, that I now have, my individuated soul. And that's why the Soul is a part of me and I am a part of the Soul. Now un-imagine being the soul.

Listening to your soul is not listening with your ears. The soul speaks to you in the language of feelings. You notice your feelings as you experience them in your body. When you pay attention to your feelings you are listening to your soul. Your soul is your truth. I like to refer to it as your truth detector. What is best for you is what it true for you so it is in your best interest to pay attention to your soul. As you do this on a regular basis you are doing only what is true for you and that speeds you down your path. Pay attention to your soul. Act on it with your now truth. In doing so you produce a new you.

I was ashamed of who I was being at certain times in my life. However, I learned that I would not be exactly where I am today, were it not for having gone through all that I went through, good and bad. I am perfectly where I am today because of every single thing I went through, and I had to go through all of that or I would not have gone through it. There is no need to be ashamed. God is good and everything God created is good. God does not judge. God says for me to ask only, "Am I better than I was before?"

Every desire is held with a belief that one will feel better when that desire is achieved. Experiencing world peace will be an achievement that will, indeed, have each of us feeling better.

If we are going to experience world peace, and we will, we need to fully understand what an experience is. An experience is something that has occurred or happened to us. Our lives are made up of experiences. Nothing in our lives happens without being part of an experience. And every experience is new. There are no old experiences. Every experience is a new creation. Notice I said 'a new creation'. One cannot have an old experience just as one cannot have an old creation.

Every moment is a new experience and each can be a different length of time. An experience can consist of your actions(your body), your words, thoughts, ideas,(your mind) and your feelings.(your soul). Actions of the body also include actions of each of our senses of sight, hearing, smelling, tasting, touching and knowing.

Try to remember an experience in your life from years ago. Paint a picture of it in your mind as you remember more and more pieces of it. You can see what you saw, taste what you tasted, hear what you heard, smell what you smelled and feel what you felt then. You can relive the entire experience, like it was here, again.

So how does that all happen? How can it be there years ago and also be here and now? How is remembering possible? Remembering is reliving an experience, a moment in time.

I asked, I received, and now I understand how it works. Before I asked and received, I was of the belief that my thoughts were stored in my mind. I also believed I could remember and that remembering was retrieving old thoughts from my mind. I was partially right. I believed the thoughts were stored in my mind but I had no idea where the smells, the sights, the tastes and all the rest were stored. What an interesting surprise, when, again, I learned by asking and receiving.

The mind is where the experience is stored! Not just the thoughts but the entire experience. Every experience is stored in my mind. When I remember something, I am remembering an entire experience just as that experience was the first time. My thought at the time was a member of that experience. My feeling, my action, and the actions of all of my senses were members of that experience. Re-member-ing is bringing the members of the experience back together again from the mind where they are stored.

You've lived your entire life, so far, not knowing that experiences are stored out there - in the rainbow. Therefore, you would have thought that idea untrue - until now - but it existed there the entire time.

We now know that feelings provide the drive, thoughts provide the direction, and actions provide the results. This is your soul, mind and body working in harmony, naturally. In each moment, they combine to create an experience.

Which is to say, in each moment you create an experience using your soul, your mind and your body. Each experience contains feelings, thoughts and actions. One cannot have an experience without all three as members of that experience.

As a baby, you noticed the feelings your soul sent you. You noticed them in your body where you experienced them. You acted accordingly. At that age, your mind did not get in the way as you moved along your life path. You were living your life with your soul, your body, and your mind but your body and mind were not yet fully developed. You, your soul, body and mind, were joy, a bundle of joy.

As a baby, your actions involved very little thought. You had very little in your mind to help or hinder you along your life path.

As you grew, so did your use of your mind and your free will. Somewhere between being a baby and now, you started ignoring your feelings and turned to your mind to determine your actions. By ignoring your feelings you were ignoring your soul. You were living your life with your body, and your mind. You started believing that you were your body and your mind. You had forgotten who you really were. You had forgotten the part your soul plays in your life.

Lots of people helped you forget. Your parents may have helped you the most. They did so because that is what they knew. Their parents helped them forget too. And their parents before them. This occurred around the globe. This helped everyone think, and even believe, they were right. This helped everyone live their lives and live their lies, absent good feelings. Notice the condition of the world today. The observable truth is showing us that what we have been doing for thousands of years is not working.

Today, right now, you have re-member-ed who you really are. You've gone from a two part you; body and mind, to a three part you; soul, body and mind. You've brought your soul back in as a member of who you really are.

You've gone there simply by changing your mind about who you are. You changed to a new way of thinking. By changing your mind, you changed the Mind. You are one of many who are on the way to a global shift in consciousness, a shift that will affect world peace.

Smile. When you experience that smiling, it is your experience and only yours. Nobody else can experience your smiling experience at the same time as you are experiencing it. They may, however, also be smiling and experiencing their own smiling. You, also, cannot be experiencing their smiling experience as they are.

An experience is person-specific. Two people can experience a car crash but each will have their very own experience of that car crash. Neither can experience what the other is experiencing during that car crash. Likewise, for every experience in every moment of every human beings life. Only the experiencer can experience a happening as the happening is being experienced.

Therefore, only the person experiencing a happening can truly know that happening. We may think we understand someone else's experience but we cannot **know it** as that person does. As I experience a smile, one could observe me smiling. One could not, however, observe the feeling I had. One could also not observe what I was thinking in that experience. By not knowing my feeling and my thought in that experience, others cannot know that experience as I know it. We can observe another's experience and we can think about another's experience but we cannot know it as the experiencer knows it. Your smiling experience could be observed by others. You could also observe another as they experience their smiling experience. They cannot know your experience and you cannot know theirs.

For someone else to know an experience of yours, that someone would need to be **in** you, in your cells, during that experience. They would need to be in your body to feel what you are feeling, as feeling is part of that experience. That is not possible. They would need to be in your mind to think what your thoughts are, as thoughts are part of that experience. That also is not possible. The same holds true for you. For you to know another's experience, you would need to be inside of their mind and body, inside them. That also is not possible.

But God was, and is in you and thereby continues to know all, even every one of your experiences.

A baby moves inside the womb. As the baby moves, the baby experiences its body moving. God, being in every cell of the baby, also experiences it. If God was not inside every part of the baby, God would not be able to experience the baby's movement at the precise time the baby was experiencing that movement.

Thoughts are energy. All energy attracts. The energy of our thoughts attract similar thoughts. In our minds, our thoughts attract like thoughts, our feelings attract like feelings, and our experiences attract like experiences.

Each of the members of an experience are some kind of energy. Each of those energies are attracting like energies. If an experience had joy it in, then it attracts joy. If an experience had anger in it, then it attracts anger. Experiences with blame, shame, depression, guilt, rage or fury attract experiences with blame, shame, depression, guilt, rage or fury. Experiences with love, joy, peace, unity, oneness or harmony attract experiences with love, joy, peace, unity, oneness or harmony.

Living Consciously

The simple process of placing higher(love or a derivative) energy feelings into your experiences, consciously, has you living every moment consciously, and living your life consciously. It is the ultimate "Ask and you shall receive!" What you think about you bring about.

When you want to live a better life, attract better experiences into your life. Store better experiences and you attract even better experiences. Attracting better experiences allows you to live the better experiences that you have attracted.

Emotions are energy in motion. There are only two emotions, fear and love. All human actions are motivated by emotions. Every human thought, and every human action, is based in either love or fear. There is no other human motivation, and all other ideas are but derivatives of these two. Every thought, word, or deed is based on one emotion or the other. You have no choice about this because there is nothing else from which to choose. You, however, have free will to choose either one of these.

As a feeling arrives at the sensors of our cells, the energy of the feeling is transferred to those cells. The cells are excited or moved to act. This action is energy in motion or emotions. It is feeling experienced.

I want to emphasize the importance of feeling even more. Let me explain. I experienced a moment of joy as I read an email my daughter sent me. She was delighted with the information I had sent her. I experienced a feeling of joy in that moment. Then I stopped to consider the entirety of the experience of that moment. When I experienced that feeling of joy, in that moment, God also experienced that exact same feeling of joy. In that moment, God and I shared that same feeling of joy. God did not share one feeling of joy and me another. It was that one feeling, that single feeling of joy that we both shared. God and I shared that one feeling of joy, together, at the same time, in that exact same experience.

We not only shared the feeling of joy but we shared the entire experience of that moment. God could not feel what I feel, as I feel it, without being in my body, in each of my cells, where the feeling sensors are located. By being in there, God can feel what I feel as I feel it. By being in there, I can create, or co-create, the experience in the moment. From now on, I can consciously create joyful moments knowing I am creating joyful moments for God to experience as well. Wow! Is that cool or what? What a great feeling! What a great experience!

Knowing now that we create our own experiences, we soon come to the realization that we created every single experience of our life. It is impossible to make a mistake in the process of creation. There are therefore no mistakes in any of our past experiences. All experiences are created without mistakes. This means there were no mistakes in our past either because our past is a sequence of our experiences. You are exactly where you are in this moment because of the experiences of your life, which you created. Everything that you create is perfect just as it is and that includes you and your experiences.

You have the power to create what you wish to experience in your life. So, go ahead and create each new experience for the rest of your life. Create your life as you want it to be. You are wondrous magnificence.

You can re-live and modify, or re-member, a 'past' experience, in a current experience. You can basically re-create it. It was your creation in the first place. So, ask the mind for the experience you wish to modify. It will be remembered into its original creation and presented to you. Bring more joy to the experience and you have modified it.

Once this moment has passed, this newly created experience is stored just like the first one. That newly modified experience is now stored with the modifications you made to it. Now you have two experiences, almost identical, except for the modifications to the second. One cannot create two identical experiences because one is creating an experience every time one is having an experience and one cannot create a twin, exactly, or it would be a duplication and would not be a creation.

An emotion is energy in motion. An emotion summons energy. An emotion indicates how much energy you are summoning. The higher the emotion the more energy it is summoning. Strong emotions mean your desires are powerfully focused and that summons a great deal of energy towards your desire. You can decide how much energy to put into motion and then place that emotion into an experience.

We only have so much emotional energy each day. Unless, of course, we don't! Do we have the same amount of energy every day? We take in food, oxygen and water and our body converts it to physical energy. By using that energy, we put that energy into motion. The importance of this process grows with the possibility of modifying emotions stored with each experience.

Attracting energy that is higher adds to your current energy level. Attracting energy that is lower weights on your current energy level. We all want more energy to do and be more. By consciously adding a member to each experience that has a higher energy than our current level, increases the energy that we receive by attraction.

Think of a time when you were angry with something or someone in your life. Maybe it was when you were a kid, a teenager, or even an adult. Next, think about why you had that anger at that time. In that moment, in that experience, you injected anger into that experience not knowing that that feeling of anger would be stored with that experience for the rest of time. Worse yet, that feeling of anger would attract even more feelings of anger to you from that moment forward.

Now that you know how this works, you can change the way you do things, now, and the future. From here forward, you can direct your life, by choice, not by chance. You can choose to add a good or a better feeling to the moment you are in. You are choosing. You have the free will to choose. You were born with it. Choose, if you feel like it!

Attraction works on everything. When you expect something, it is on the way. When you believe something, it is on the way. When you fear something, it is on the way. If you don't like what you are attracting, change who you are being.

Much of what you do today is re-acting. You created an action years ago, many of them, and have recreated those same actions many times over since then. Your mind has those actions stored, each stored as part of an experience.

What we experience, we become. What we experience becomes a part of our mind and thus a part of who we are. For example, think about smiling at a friend. Hold that thought for a moment and then let it go. Now think about what you are reading here. That smile experience is now stored in your mind. You have just become a person who owns that stored smile experience. You have become that. What you experience, you become.

You did that. Nobody did that for you or to you. You are now that. You became that when you created that experience. You created that experience, in its entirety. You are a creator. God created you that way. God created you with the ability to create, and while you are doing your creating, for you to also experience your creation, and in that process, allow God to experience you creating.

Once you know that you really are mind, body and soul you become that. You then wish to create something, heal something or experience something to be who you really are. Everything that happens or occurs in your life is an opportunity to create, heal or experience something. Within every happening and every occurrence you can experience who you really are.

Hug someone. God experiences you hugging that person. God also experiences that person experiencing receiving your hug. God receives a double whammy. God experiences both hugs, the senders hug and the receivers hug. Think about that and your moment after the hug will have another good feeling in it. Do the same with joy. Bring joy into another person's life and God will experience your giving and the other person's receiving joy. The same holds true for love, peace, harmony, unity, oneness and on and on.

Even more changes have occurred in your consciousness while reading this chapter. You are propelling yourself, even faster, on your path to experiencing world peace. Notice, again, who you are being, and how that has shifted from who you were being before. Notice, how you are better than you were before.

Living Consciously

This chapter takes you through yet another consciousness shift, this time about living consciously vs unconsciously. You will learn that you can choose to live your life consciously.

A life is made up of one experience followed by another experience, followed by another, and another, and so on. We live in each of our experiences. We are the lump sum total of all of the combined experiences of our life up to this moment. The question is, *"How much of our life have we lived consciously?"* Where has that gotten us? Are we where we want to be? Is the world the way we want it to be? Are we happy? Do we feel good? Are we experiencing world peace?

Consciously living our lives is consciously living every moment of our lives. By being conscious of what is happening in each moment, and making a conscious decision to change it, or leave it as is, we are consciously living every moment. We are then living by choice and not by chance. We are using our free will to go higher, to be more love.

When we pay attention to the thought we are having in a moment, we are living in the moment. When we notice the feeling we receive in a moment, we are living in the moment. When we make a conscious decision to change the thought, or leave it as is, we are living in the moment. By living in the moment, we are choosing to go higher, consciously, instead of leaving that to chance. Living our lives by chance is gambling that we will go higher.

Humans who do not feel good will, by their very nature, eventually crave good feelings. All people want to feel better. It is in their very nature to do so. No human can get around this. It is in their nature and one cannot change one's nature. As more people understand this truth they will develop a completely different understanding of, and respect for, feelings. Removing the craving for good feelings will reduce suicides, terrorism, crime, hate, war, riots, depression, obesity, destruction, blame and so many more.

The people with an absence of good feelings did not have an absence of good feelings when they were born. The babies lived in the moment and then later learned not to. Now we live with the observable truth that what they learned since then is what we taught them.

We are now faced with another choice. We can now choose to dwell on all the bad that was learned or we can choose to live in the moment we are in, and thereby know we are moving higher. Dwelling on our past is dwelling on our past experiences. Just as you cannot change an experience in your past you cannot change your past. Consider that you created each of your experiences. To change them would mean you would need to un-create them. Good luck with that!

God knows that every moment that happened in your life was perfect. It got your life exactly where your life is right now, which is in perfect alignment with your life plan. God's concern in this moment is, "Are you better than you were before?"

For centuries humans have treated the absence of world peace as a military problem, a political problem or an economic problem. It is none of these. It is a spiritual problem. Humanity's struggle is a struggle for the mind. Only by changing people's minds can victory in the struggle to bring peace, unity and harmony to humanity be claimed. This will only occur once people understand their problem is a spiritual problem. Once this is understood, then military, economic and political tools can and will be used to help solve the problem. Everything in our lives will be rearranged to become part of the solution. Many will be asking and receiving guidance and become part of the solution.

You will become part of the solution. People will try to get into your mind but you will now control everything going in and out of your mind. Religious leaders, educators, politicians, and many others, will attempt to force their beliefs on us. They will continue to use fear, as before, but now you notice that this does not feel good and you will no longer allow it. Their use of fear to control your mind stops working. You now control your mind and therefore control you.

If you were looking for someone to blame for the absence of peace, you would find that everyone is to blame, and no one is to blame. This is not a process that can be improved by blaming. Blaming never improves life. This is a process of becoming aware of, building a belief of and finally knowing, again, for the first time.

Everyone, including religious leaders, have been misled for centuries. They will know this for the first time because their minds will know it for the first time. They will know it again because their souls knew this truth before. They needed to control you and to control you they needed to control your mind. To control your mind they needed to control your fear. They got you to believe that they were right and you were wrong and if you didn't believe that you were going to be punished.

It started with physical punishment which later evolved to punishment created in your mind. The fear of burning in hell is a great motivator. The one problem they have always faced is that by using fear it never felt good. They were also faced with our trillions of cells instinctually wanting, longing for, that good feeling.

Freedom is not something we earn nor is it something that can be granted to others. It is the essence of life, what you are.

God is freedom. Since we are a part of God we are also part of freedom. We are inherently free.

The soul is freedom. We have been fighting for freedom for centuries, not realizing that freedom is not something one fights for. To win that fight, one would need to be fighting with one's soul, which is a fight with oneself, which one cannot win.

This freedom extends into allowing, being free to think what we choose to think. Each thought we have is a choice. We are free to have a thought just the way we put it together or to change it to our liking and then add it to our mind. To our liking is usually done with the **thought** of whether the thought was right or wrong. It is never right or wrong. It is always a case of feeling good or not.

We've covered 'ask and you shall receive' earlier in this book and you now more fully understand what that is. Did you know you can also request an improved state of being? Every point of consciousness can request an improved state of being, and get it. That includes the consciousness of a cell in your body. Requests do not get in line to be granted. All requests are granted. All desires are answered. Your request does not compete with others. Your request is granted upon arrival.

Include it in your attention and it becomes part of your vibration. What are you putting your attention on? If you expect something, it is on its way, when you believe something, it is on its way, and when you fear something, it is on its way. Choose to change what is on its way to you.

I prefer good things on the way. I will consciously expect and believe that whatever is good for me is on its way to me because I will consciously choose my thoughts that feel good.

First you experience. Then you respond to it. Become a deliberate creator, by deciding to direct your thoughts. Use focus and practice to choose different thoughts. If you want things to change to different things, you must first think different thoughts. The one thing that prevents you from receiving something you desire is that your habit of thought is different from your desire.

Here is the greatest challenge human beings face. Stop making things up. Be in the moment. Be here now. Allow the gift you sent yourself in this moment. This is the purpose of all of life. Life is a process of ongoing and never ending re-creation.

Remove our thoughts about who we think we are and then we'll know we really are soul, mind and body. We are part and parcel of God. Instead of pre-serving who we think we are, we must pre-serve who we really are. Pre-serving a creator infused human being is pre-serving us to a higher level of consciousness. This cannot bring us down, as our thoughts can. It is a faster and a higher energy than we receive when we pre-serve only to our thoughts.

When all is said, and done, imagine how you would feel living in a time of world peace while knowing you had a part in creating it. Happiness would be a big part of every moment. And after all, isn't that what we've all wanted all along?

Planning a book on achieving world peace has its challenges. One challenge is learning the paths required to get to world peace. Another is believing and eventually knowing I am on the correct path to attain my goal. The biggest challenge, so far, has been living the directions I am suggesting will get us to world peace. How can I expect others to go there if I have not gone there myself? If I want to have you experience feeling good in every moment of your life how can I help you get there when I am not there myself? I am practicing, in many moments, more than I was before.

Where does one start? What are the steps from here to there? How does one write a book on how to achieve world peace when one does not have a complete plan on how to do that? From my knowledge, it has not been done before on this earth. I cannot ask another person on earth what that was like because nobody on earth has that experience. For many of my answers, I've asked and I've received. I'm also getting better at that. I'm better than I was before. I don't have all the answers. What I do know, without doubt, is that since starting this project, I've had many, many moments in which I've experienced a good feeling while having the thought that I was better than I was before.

For most of our lives we've lived with focus on thoughts from our mind and actions of our body. We operated at a very low vibrational level as we were ignoring our soul. From here forward we will live our lives focused on our feelings and stop ignoring our soul. This will move us to a higher vibrational level of consciousness.

The higher self is not up, or further up, but rather of a higher vibrational energy. This does not place me, or you, higher or lower than anyone else. You (body+soul+mind) are simply existing at a higher vibrational level than before. You are better than you were before.

When enough people think thoughts in alignment with enough other people, a tipping point is reached in which the rest of the non-aligned people will become aligned in their thinking as well. Elevate the conversation.

For example, as more people consciously think higher thoughts of peace, aligning them with many other people thinking thoughts of peace, eventually a tipping point is reached in which the rest of the non-peace thinking people will become aligned in peace thinking as well. This will make world peace possible even without people of terror becoming instruments of peace. You have choice. People of terror will not.

Separate yourself from current events. Changing all the events in the world will not bring about world peace. Changing consciousness will. Move **feelings** from being the **least important** decision maker in your life to being the **most important** decision maker in your life.

You are not in charge of how much love is in your soul. You are not in charge of how much love is in your body. You are, however, in charge of how much love is in your mind. You are therefore in charge of how much love you are being.

Every struggle that people have is a struggle with what people have placed in their minds. The struggle is never with their soul or with their body although it could be a struggle with what they have placed in their minds about their soul or their body.

Do you ever feel like a failure? There is no failure! There are only experiences. And each of them is created and a creation cannot be a failure. Experiences are, however, lessons. You learn from those experiences, or you don't learn from them. Either way, God is teaching each of us through our experiences. It's God's favorite way of communicating with us and is many times the answer portion of ask and you shall receive.

You're either open to learning from your experiences or you're not. Either way, it is your free will choice that you and you alone are making. Changing your beliefs from being a failure to being a success is a change in consciousness that will take you closer to inner peace. It's as simple as changing your mind and it will simply change your life. Make the change, consciously.

For centuries many have attempted to describe God. All of the descriptions created by man minimize who and what God is. God is so much more.

So, let's get over ourselves, and our need to create an accurate description of who and what God is. Allow God to be, just as God decided to be, nothing more, nothing less. No matter your description of God, God will still be whatever God was before you described God. God is what God is!

To have an experience with a thought that God is love, joy, peace, harmony, unity and oneness feels good. To have an experience with a thought that God is fear, anger, greed, shame, duality, chaos does not feel good. Think about the things you've been taught about God that are now stored in your mind. Change your mind about all of the bad things you were taught about God and notice how much better you feel. You will be changing your consciousness about that man-made God and know God, as what God really is.

If you learned that by taking two extra breaths of air every hour you would extend your life by two years, would you create a habit of taking those two extra breaths? What if twenty extra breaths extended your life twenty extra years? Would that convince you to create the habit? What about creating a habit of changing your thoughts consciously every moment? Would it be worth the work required to develop the habit? What would motivate you to create that habit?

On earth, today, every hour, 400 children are dying of starvation. How do you think the creator feels as we allow each of these children to starve? How do you feel? Do you think those children were brought into this world to experience starvation? How do their parents feel? How would you feel if you were one of those parents? If you were God, what would you do? You are not God but you are a creator! Are you willing to create a new consciousness, in you, knowing that it could lead to feeding the world, thus stopping 400 children per hour from dying of starvation?

Allow consciousness change. Your body and soul are that consciousness already and need not make that change. Your mind is the only place where a consciousness change is needed in order for you to participate in being an instrument of creating world peace.

Consciousness is very powerful. So powerful in fact that all events, happenings, occurrences are created out of it. There is individual consciousness and there is group consciousness as when two or more are gathered in his name and finally there is mass consciousness. Individual is powerful enough but imagine when groups unleash their creative energy. And mass consciousness is so powerful it can create events and circumstances affecting the whole world and may result in planetary consequences.

Around the world today we have a consciousness that it is someone else who is responsible, or at fault, for us not having world peace. That consciousness includes blaming others for what they are doing to cause the absence of world peace. This is an example of mass consciousness creating what mass consciousness can.

In this chapter, you learned how to live a life of conscious action. You also learned why you no longer need to live the life of unconscious reaction you have been living. Your conscious actions are now contributing even more to that mass consciousness shift.

Ask And You Shall Receive

This chapter takes you through yet more consciousness shift. You will learn how 'ask and you shall receive' works and how you can make it work for you.

I can ask and I can receive. I did ask and I did receive. I continue to ask and I continue to receive. I have not perfected this process for myself but I practice it much more than I did before.

You can ask and you can receive. Many do not believe that they can ask and receive. If you want to know what is true for you, look to how you feel about it.

People have told me that God does not talk to me nor does God talk to anyone else. They say he only talks to some special hand-picked individuals, like Jesus and Moses and several others. When I asked God who he talks to I got a completely different answer. God says the question is not to whom he talks but who listens to him. God says he talks to everyone and does so all the time. God also says we should exchange the word talk with the word communicate, as it is a much better, fuller and more accurate word. God adds that he rarely communicates by words alone.

God's common forms of communications:

- Through feelings:

To know what is true for you about something, notice how you feel about it.

- Through thoughts:

Thoughts and feelings can occur at the same time but are not the same thing. Thoughts can include pictures and images making them very effective for communicating.

- Through experiences:

Experiences are a grand communicator.

- Through words:

When thoughts and feelings fail to communicate the message, God uses words. Words are the most often misunderstood, the most open to misinterpretation and the least effective communicator.

The supreme irony is that we place very little value on an experience we receive from God but place much value on words we've heard from others. We simple discard the experience and hang on to the words instead. We should be discarding the words and hang on to the experience.

You will not miss God's messages if you truly listen. Once you hear his messages you can no longer ignore them. In the past you prayed to God, talked to God, pleaded with God and implored God. Even here in this book God is communicating to you.

God also says:

- All people are special.

- There is no person more special than another.

- All moments are golden.

- There is no time more special than another.

For many people listening to what someone else thinks they heard God say they do not have to think at all. If they were to acknowledge receiving a message from God directly they would be responsible for interpreting it. They would rather allow someone else to interpret the message even if that interpretation is wrong.

Some people are willing to actually listen to God. That is the only reason they hear more from God than others. They are open to the communication even when it seems scary, or crazy or even wrong. Especially when something seems wrong, listen to God for answers.

You can continue to act on only what you know. This has been done since the beginning of time. Observe where that has taken mankind. It's time to move from relying on what you know to instead noticing and relying on your feelings and experiences. You could do what great scientists do which is to set aside all you know and start over. You can do it if you have a willingness and ability to not be right.

If you believe and told yourself you already know God, you cannot really know God. If you've already heard God, you cannot really hear God.

If you know you can communicate with God, you are listening to your soul. If you think you can't communicate with God, you are listening to your mind. The soul is truth, and yet you can choose to believe your mind.

As you know, God is love, joy, harmony, unity, oneness, peace and so very much more. Do you think God would go ahead and create a thing as advanced and wondrously magnificent as the human body and then not give it a way to communicate with God? God communicates with everything. Every single thing! Most everything else listens. We have listened too, just not to the degree that we could.

You are responsible for communicating directly with God. Do you understand that? You are response-able for communicating directly with God. In other words, you are able to provide response to communications with God. This is not something you are forced to do. You have been given free will and you can choose.

Ask and you shall receive has worked for me in many ways. Try it yourself. Ask God a question you do not have an answer to. You can ask by stating the question out loud. You can ask by simply thinking the question. You can ask in whatever way you want and God will be listening. God can hear you no matter how you ask because, as you know, God is in you at the cellular level. Asking is the easy part. Every human on earth is also receiving answers, all the time.

The bigger question is, are you ready to receive an answer? Are you listening? Are you open to receiving an answer from God? Do you believe that God could or would speak to you? When you receive an answer 'out of the blue', do you doubt that you received it or do you now doubt that it works that way. When you received your answer 'out of the blue' did you think it was coming from somewhere other than from God?

Could you have a conversation with God? Could anyone? If not, why not? If so, are you? How could someone like Neale Donald Walsch have a conversation with God? He did and he wrote about those conversations in his series of books titled *'Conversations With God'*. So if Mr Walsch could have a conversation with God, then why couldn't you? Why couldn't I? Why couldn't everyone? Or, are we all having conversations with God and just don't know it? Are we all having conversations with God and don't think of them as conversations? Read his books and notice the clarity in everything that God says. Read his books and notice how you feel as you read them.

I hope each and every one of you questions what is said here and come to your own conclusion. If it feels right for you, then you know. If it does not feel right for you, then you know. Either way it is your feeling that you are receiving from your soul, letting you know if you are on your right path or not. My path is not for you. Your path is not for me. We are all to experience our own path.

You are asking when you:

- Give attention to something you desire.
- Give attention to something you do not desire.
- Try to figure something out.

Jesus of Nazareth spoke often of 'ask and you shall receive'. He did not say, "Hey Joe, you can ask and you shall receive". "And you Judy, You can also ask and you shall receive." Jesus simply said, "Ask and you shall receive." It was not a gift to some and not to others. It is simply a gift to all. God did not create two classes of people and give one this power and the other not. God also does not judge people and decide which ones to give this opportunity to. The statement is, "Ask and you shall receive."

Prayer is talking. Religions promote it. Talking is not a threat to religions. Meditation is listening. Religions do not promote it. Listening is a threat to religions. Religions want you to listen to them as the source of your information and they fear your listening to God as your source of information will expose their deception. Prayer is consciously 'sending' energy and meditation is consciously 'receiving' energy. Ask and you shall receive, is sending and receiving energy.

Many people think their prayers go unanswered. Here is an example of what is likely happening with an unanswered prayer. Let's say you are praying to find your ideal job. The job you want is at a company you'd like to work for, doing what you'd love to do and comes with a generous salary. This is your thought as you pray. It is however not your controlling thought. The controlling thought, or thought behind the thought, is that you won't get that job because you aren't good enough, you're always passed over, and this kind of thing always happens to you. Your thoughts about not being worthy are stronger than your thoughts about receiving the job. Control your thoughts behind the thought and you'll control your prayers.

To control your prayers, start by writing them down. Make a list of the things you pray for. When you've finished writing your list, read your prayers out loud. Read one and then think about what your thought behind that prayer is or may be. Chances are you'll discover that each of your prayers that isn't being answered has a thought behind it that is stopping you from having your prayer answered. When you figure out the thought behind a prayer in your list, write it next to that prayer. Do that for every prayer in your list.

You'll uncover every thought behind every thought you're having as you are praying. Now that you know those thoughts behind the thoughts you can get rid of them. Do that by thinking the opposite of what you've written down. Your prayers will be answered. Do this every time you pray.

Every thought you have is a form of asking. You need to spend a ton of time listening, truly listening, allowing God to answer, not on your terms, but on God's terms, which is the terms of your soul.

Listen to the Lord. Listen to the word of the Lord. It does not say listen to the written word of the Lord. It does not say listen to the words others have put on paper. It does not say listen to the word others have translated, filtered or otherwise determined what was said. It says, "Listen to the Lord" and it says "Listen to the word of the Lord." To me that means exactly what it says. Notice that the two statements differ. Listen to the Lord means you can listen to the Lord in whatever form that may take. Listen to the word of the Lord means you can listen to the word of the Lord in whatever form it comes in. It may come in the form of a song. It may come in the form of a billboard. It may come in the form of a newspaper article or TV show. God speaks to us in many ways. Listen because God speaks to you. Be the cause of God speaking to you.

Notice, that when you are reading a question, you are also asking. Notice how you feel during that experience. You may also be receiving an answer to what is in that moment your question.

In this chapter, you learned some of the ways 'ask and you shall receive' can work for you. This book reflects many examples of how 'ask and you shall receive' has worked for me. With all of the 'receiving' I've done, think about all of the good feelings I've experienced in that process. You too can do this, and more.

You Are A Creation Machine

In this chapter you will learn how you already do so much creating that you are considered a creation machine by none other than God. It will open your mind to vast possibilities and opportunities wherein you will create even more.

You may find it hard to believe but you are a creation machine. You are continually creating in every moment. Your soul, body and mind are creating, and therefore, you are also creating. You are not God but of God, so you can do this.

First and foremost, you create your own experiences. We covered experiences earlier in this book. Try to stop yourself from creating your own present experience. You cannot! This is not a choice you were given. These creations, every moment, are built right into you, a part of your very nature. You create experiences naturally, along with many other creations. This gives you experience at creating. You may not have thought of it that way before but that is your truth whether you allow that truth into your mind or whether you deny it. It is there, every moment, happening. Think about it or not it occurs, you create. If you don't think about it as it occurs, you are creating unconsciously, without your mind as an active participant. If you think about it as it occurs, you are creating consciously, with your mind as an active participant. Either way, you are creating.

Some of the things you create, consciously or unconsciously, are: sounds, movements, smiles, body heat, sweat, carbon dioxide, footsteps, hand gestures, urine, frowns, tears, feelings, thoughts, ideas, mental images, joy and desires. These are just some examples of what you are creating, naturally. Notice your thoughts as you read this! Read this again, and notice your feelings as you read this!

You create happiness when you feel you are on your soul path.

Your thoughts are pure vibration, and they can and do create matter! Thoughts are mental constructions, made up creations of your mind. All that now exists was once imagined. What you wish to exist must first be imagined.

Notice it says 'wish' and not 'want'. Check your use of language and change it where necessary. Change from using the word **want**. When you **want** something, you cannot also **have** something. While you are wanting you cannot also be having the same thing. If you had something you would not be wanting something. Instead of wanting **something**, which would indicate you don't have it, be grateful for having it or having it be on its way to you. In this way, ask and you shall receive kicks into gear and is active in making it happen. You are manifesting it into your life instead of manifesting **wanting** into your life.

Strong emotions mean your desires are powerfully focused and that summons a great deal of energy towards your desire.

This quote is from *"Conversations With God"* by Neale Donald Walsch

"You might call the three energies of you, thought, word and action. All three put together produce a result, which is called a feeling, or experience. Your soul is the sum total of every feeling you've ever had. Your awareness of some of these is called your memory. When you have a memory, you are said to re-member. That is, to put back together. To reassemble the parts.

When you reassemble all of the parts of you, you will have re-membered who you really are.

The process of creation starts with thoughts, an idea, conception, visualization. Everything you see was once someone's idea. Nothing exists in your world that did not first exist as pure thought.

Thought is the first level of creation.

Next comes the word. Everything you say is a thought expressed. It is creative and sends forth creative energy into the universe. Words are more dynamic, and some might say creative, than thought, because words are a different level of vibration from thought. They disrupt, change, alter or affect, the universe with greater impact.

Words are the second level of creation.

Next comes action.

Actions are words moving. Words are thoughts expressed. Thoughts are ideas formed. Ideas are energies come together. Energies are forces released. Forces are elements existent. Elements are particles of God, portions of all, the stuff of everything."

Now you, the you that is your mind, body, soul, can choose to know, without doubt.

Mind: Thoughts - convinced that one knows.

Body: Feelings - the sense of knowing is activated.

Soul: Actions - has sent the feeling of knowing to the body.

Unity: It all happens in the moment, the same experience.

Oneness: All are acting as one, the catalyst for creation, manifesting.

The experience stored in the mind has a tremendous energy, attracting what is known, to be made manifest.

Notice the **soul action**, above, stating that **the feeling of knowing** is sent to the body. We've all experienced a moment in which we had a **sense of knowing** something, and thereby knowing that something for sure. That feeling helped us to **feel** certain we knew **that something** without doubt. Without this feeling of knowing, one may have doubt. With this feeling, there is a sense of knowing, without doubt.

This knowing is stronger than having thoughts or a belief of knowing which comes only from the mind. Each sense of knowing is experienced in the body in the moment the feeling the soul has sent is felt or experienced in the body. You cannot allow or disallow your soul from doing this, from sending you these feelings. Your soul participates either way. You can, however, choose to notice your soul's participation in your experience of sensing your knowing.

You can use your imagination to create anything. Your imagination works both ways. You not only interpret energy, you create it. Imagination is a function of your mind, which is one third of your three-part being. In your mind, you imagine something and it begins to take physical form. The longer you image it, and the more of you who image it, the more physical that form becomes, until the increasing energy you have given it literally bursts into light, flashing an image of itself into your reality.

You then see the image and decide what it is. This is the process of your life. You are applying it every day. This is what is happening. The only question is whether you apply it consciously or unconsciously, whether you are the effect of the process or you are the cause of the process. In everything, be the cause.

Children understand this perfectly. Ask a child why they are doing something and they reply, "just because". That is the only reason to do anything. Be the cause of each of your experiences. Consciously cause each of your experiences to be of your making of your creation. By being the cause of each experience, with conscious thought, you choose your path. Compare that to not being the cause of each experience. Unconsciously you choose your path by chance. Either way you are choosing. Choose consciously and you speed your way on your path. Choose unconsciously and you slow your way on your path. Choose! Just be the cause!

Natural law requires the body, mind, and soul to be united in thought, word, and action for the process of creation to work. Remember this: the soul creates, the mind reacts. It is obvious that the perfect creative situation is to really, really want something that you truly believe is possible.

Everything is a creation. It must be, as God says, or there would be duplication and nothing is duplication or it would not be a creation. It is a creation, or it cannot be. Everything is a creation.

It is known that no two snowflakes are the same. Many have heard this and believed it to be true but have not given it much thought. Consider that every raindrop is a new creation different from every other raindrop in a rainfall. Consider that every raindrop is also different than every raindrop that has ever fallen. That is hard to comprehend just as it is hard to comprehend how each snowflake can be different than every other snowflake.

Consider that each blade of grass on earth is different than all the others and that each is also a new creation. Each leaf on all the trees on earth is different, each a creation. Each granule of earth is different, each a creation. This is true for everything, not just on earth but everywhere.

One million skin cells of your body are replaced every hour, and no skin cell is the same as any skin cell ever created in the universe. Something greater than me, greater than us, is handling these creations to insure each is a new creation.

That someone, or something, is a creator. Notice I said is **a** creator and I did not say is **the** creator. Yes, God is the creator. But God is not the only creator. I am a creator. You are a creator. God created me to be a creator. God created you to be a creator. God desires to experience the act of creation through me, through you, through every body.

God gave us free will to choose our beliefs. We can believe we are creators or we can choose not to believe it. We can believe it is our truth to think we are creators or we can believe it is our truth that we are not creators. We have these choices because we were given free will. We choose but truth remains the same.

But what if we found evidence that our earlier choice about this truth was not truth at all? Free will would allow us to **choose again.** Would we choose the truth or would we choose to stay with what our truth was before? We have free will to choose. We also have free will to choose again.

Remember reading earlier about God, the creator, being in each of us. When you create something, God experiences your creating that something. By experiencing your creation, God knows that experience, intimately, at the same time you do, and thereby continues to know all. Because God is in you, even at the cellular level, you cannot create without God also creating whatever it is you are creating. Some call it co-creating. In this way, God also created that something and therefore continues to create all.

I realize that it is quite a stretch to think of yourself as a creator. That is, until you realize, understand, know, you've been a creator all your life. The difference is that you now know it in your mind which is the only part of you that didn't know this all along. The body and the soul knew and now the all of you knows. You have changed only because your mind has changed, a change, by the way, which you created.

Some say that it's not really a creation if what one creates is too small and insignificant. It has to be something more substantive in order to rise to the level of creation.

To this I would reply, how small, and insignificant, was that cell which was the second cell of the creation of your body? Without that first cell, and without that first cell creating a second cell, you would not be. None of us would be. And yet you, the you that at that moment was your mind, your soul and your one cell body, created that second cell. So, with that in mind, did you create you? And yet you deny that you are a creator while your body goes on creating new cells every moment.

Put your body under stress and you put God under stress. As you experience stress God also experiences that stress. Remove the stress you are experiencing and you remove the stress God is experiencing. You'll appreciate it and so will God.

God created everything. If there is a thing, then that thing had to be created or it wouldn't be a thing at all. We often think of things God created as things we can see, such as the earth, trees, grass, insects, birds, ants, animals, lakes, rivers, flowers, butterfly's, air, water and rock. Then we have what God created beyond what is on our earth such as the stars, sun, moon, planets and the rest of the universe. But what about the things we cannot see such as smell, taste and sound. These things also had to be created by God or they would not be, either. Simply by their being, they had to be created to exist.

Then we have the somewhat unexpected. What about thoughts and feelings? Were thoughts and feelings also created by God or by us? If they exist, and if they came to you, they had to come from somewhere. Do you doubt that thoughts and feelings exist?

My experiences produced my desires. Experiences create all desires. Notice that, in that sentence, **Experiences create** . . .', that even the experiences, that I create, create. I am a creation machine! My experiences were exactly perfect for me to get to exactly where I am today, therefore, the desires I now have are perfect for me today. Ditto for you!

That's why movies can be such negative influences on a human's life. The observer observes what he or she experiences as real versus that it is simply acting as if. It's interesting that actors are paid to provide a distortion of the here and now. And yet the best way for us to achieve a goal is to **act as if** it is here and now. To create in my life I **must** pretend as if, or act as if, it is already here and now. If I truly believe, with feeling, that it is already here and now, it is. We have had this example in front of us all these years, since people starting pretending or acting as if.

As you achieve more your ability to reach for more expands. The value in recognizing emotions and then consciously offering thoughts to deliberately produce better feeling emotions is truly what deliberate creation is.

What is deliberately producing better feeling emotions? What is an emotion? Emotion is energy in motion. How does one put energy in motion?

The energy we take in and the energy we give back, which is all of life itself, is simply moved around in what we call life. It is life. It is part of our life or we have no life. By breathing more, we can generate more energy of life and change our lives in the process.

By adding energy to our feelings or creating emotions we change our next moment and thereby change our life. We can build stronger emotions, thereby building stronger life energy, and create some high energy in our lives.

What will change in my life if I agree to consciously change all of my angry emotions into better feeling emotions? I will deliberately produce better feeling emotions.

An emotion is a feeling experienced. A feeling is sent from the soul to the body where it is experienced. In that moment, you experience it for the first time. After that moment has been experienced, the experience is sent to the mind where it is stored, where it attracts like experiences, and where it can be recalled.

Now that I know what I now know, I can take that feeling, that emotion, and change it to a better feeling emotion. When I do this consciously, I deliberately create a better experience and then store this improved feeling, emotion, experience, in the mind and allow it to attract better feeling experiences for me. It contains a better feeling, a stronger feeling, than the previous experience, and therefore attracts improved experiences to me.

The experience contains the feeling that was present in the moment of the experience. That feeling could have been a bad feeling or a good feeling, but it was an experienced feeling in that moment. When the experience is recalled the feeling again surfaces along with the other members of the experience. Deliberately changing the feeling to a better feeling emotion is deliberate creation. You are deliberately creating a better life for yourself. You are deliberately creating better energy in your life. Living a higher energy life allows you to give a higher energy life to others. Deliberately improving your life deliberately improves other lives as well.

I want to deliberately create a better feeling emotional life for myself, but I also want to hang on to the past which has served me during all those years of being right. Being right is important to me. I have a strong need to be right! What if my entire life has been wrong? What if all of our lives have been wrong? Would it be so bad to admit that if that is all it took to start the world on the path to world peace.

I lose if I continue to be right. So does the world, as each of us is oneness with it.

As humans, we create many things using the energies we are. Humans created the house you live in, the meals you eat, the clothes you wear. They used the energy of their minds, their bodies, and tools, which they also created. Humans created the car you drive or the bus or train you ride. Humans created the TV you watch, the wrist watch, the phone and so many other things too numerous to list here.

Only a small percentage of humans have created matter. To create matter one must use the mind, body and soul together, in unity and oneness. Most of us do not know how to do that and therefore don't even try. To create matter, you must have a clear picture in 'mind' of what you are creating. Your mind must be clear of any doubt that you can do this. You must believe this in you to the point you have a knowingness inside you, your body, that you can do this. This knowingness is a feeling experienced in your body. This knowingness is a feeling sent by your soul. The soul knows. The soul also does the creating, when you are successful in your creation, which is at the moment you allow it.

There is no future, until you create it, in the moment, and then it is no longer the future. There is only possibility.

Psychologically, you will find it much easier to 'add onto' than to create out of thin air.

All events in your life are created by you unconsciously.

You are being with God! It is impossible to not be, so why consider it, but instead, allow it, since it is natural. You have God's help in all you do. God can create without you but you cannot create without God as God is in you. To create with God, choose to.

No two snowflakes are the same because it is impossible for them to be. Creation is not duplication. Having two snowflakes the same would mean there was duplication and that cannot be. Each snowflake is a creation. No two persons, thoughts or relationships are alike. Everything in the universe exists in singular form.

With focused thought for seventeen seconds a second matching vibration becomes activated. By doing this deliberately I am creating that second vibration. Following that, if I stay on focus for sixty eight seconds or more I create vibration powerful enough to start manifestation. I cannot think about the results of my focused thought as that would halt the manifestation process. I must focus on my feelings and let them lead the way.

It becomes obvious that the perfect creative situation is to really, really want something that you truly believe is possible.

You may attempt to create something but are unable to do so. Your desire may have too great of a dramatic vibrational difference to be attracted or delivered to you. You cannot attract desires of a dramatic different vibration. To move up the vibrational scale, be consciously aware of the way you feel. The feeling tells you which way you are moving on the scale. Moving up the scale produces a good feeling. Moving down the scale does not produce a good feeling. The more in vibrational harmony you are with who you really are, the better you feel.

Vibrational activation occurs within you. How? **All that we can attract must be attracted through our experiences.** That's how attraction works. The vibrational **activation** occurs when we are preparing to experience an experience. We can call in a high energy feeling to accompany the experience so that the experience goes into the mind and attracts to us at a high level of attraction. Because the vibrational level of energy is activated in the current experience one can say the vibrational activation occurs within you.

The tools of creation are:	
• Thought	Attracted from the mind
• Word	The spoken word. Speak and it shall be done onto you.
• Deed	The action you take

Think. Speak. Do.

This must include belief, knowing, a gut level clarity, a total certainty, a complete acceptance as reality of something, a come from a place of knowing, an intense and incredible gratitude, thankfulness in advance, taking for granted not just condoned but encouraged. This is a sure sign of mastery. All masters know in advance that the deed has been done.

Be wisdom, and you will have it.

You must find ways of holding yourself consistently in vibrational harmony with your desires in order to receive their manifestation. When you consciously become aligned with the well-being flow, your creative endeavors become so much more satisfying, for then there is nothing you cannot achieve. It flows, if you resist it or not.

You were created in the image and likeness of God.

God is the creator.

You are three things in one: mind, body, soul.

The creation process proceeds from these three parts of your being. You create at three levels. Your creative tools are: thought, word and deed.

Three levels of creation:

What you think of creates at one level.

What you think of and speak creates at another level.

What you think of, speak and do is made manifest in your reality.

The process of creation must include strong belief, absolute faith, knowing of a certainty, a gut level clarity and complete acceptance as reality.

This place is thankfulness in advance with an intense and incredible gratitude. Taking for granted is encouraged as all masters know in advance that the deed has been done.

Be joyful for all you create. Own it. Be thankful for it. Bless it.

This is how to manifest God's will on Earth as it is in Heaven.

In this chapter you learned how to create and how you have already been creating in each and every moment of your life. Now you know why God considers you a creation machine. Be cause of your creations.

Defining World Peace

Are you preparing yourself for world peace or are you being prepared for world peace?

Earth is without world peace today. Do not look at this as a failure, but rather, as an opportunity. You now have the opportunity to help our world attain world peace by becoming and continuing to be an instrument of peace.

Look up "world peace" on the Internet. What a collection of ideas you get. Some good and some not so good. Nowhere can I find a single article on experiencing world peace. Look up peace in a dictionary, in an encyclopedia, in books or on the Internet. The answers are as varied as the sources. There appear to be more articles on what world peace is not than what world peace is. There is no consensus on what world peace is. Why didn't more people ask God?

- Some think that peace is simply the absence or cessation of hostility.
- Some think that if we end all wars we will have world peace.
- Some say we will have world peace when we all just get along.

- Some say when we get rid of anger, and greed, and meanness, we will have world peace.
- Many say we will never have world peace.
- Some say world peace is impossible.

With these beliefs, every person is helping to manifest a world with a continued absence of world peace. Without changing those beliefs, every one of those believers will continue to be an instrument of the absence of peace. Help them change their beliefs. Pass the word and tell them about ICURY!

Where does one go to research 'experiencing world peace' when no one on earth has ever experienced world peace? Since no one has ever experienced world peace, there are no writings on that subject. Notice I used the term **experiencing world peace** instead of world peace. We could develop lots of information about world peace but until we experience it we will not **know** that experience. Therefore, we will not truly know world peace until we have experienced world peace.

Start working towards and talking about experiencing world peace. Set it as a goal. Can you suggest a loftier goal? How will you feel coming down the home stretch as all of humanity achieves world peace? Why doesn't everyone on earth have experiencing world peace as one of their goals? Help them set this as their goal. Why isn't this part of our daily conversation? Talk about it, text about it, spread the word. Why isn't this part of our daily efforts? Experience getting closer every day.

Seeking The Experience

When looking up **world peace**, most tell of **what should not be** to have world peace instead of telling what **should be.** Help people redefine, in their minds, the path to experiencing world peace. Have them ask God?

I wasn't seeking the definition of **peace**. So I didn't ask. I wasn't seeking the definition of **world peace**. So I didn't ask that question either. What I was seeking was precisely this: *What would it take for me to experience world peace?* To experience it meant that it had to exist. It also meant that it would then exist for all of us. We would all be experiencing world peace at the same time.

I asked the question. I didn't get an answer for quite some time. The answer didn't come, until I was ready for it, until I allowed it.

I was **expecting** many of the things I had read or heard about peace and world peace. I was **expecting** a long list of things that needed to be done before we could have world peace. I was **expecting** some things that would take a lot of work, and maybe even power, to achieve. While I was **expecting** these things, the answer did not come. Notice that I was **expecting** a lot of things and not **expecting** the answer. When I finally **expected** the answer, it arrived, as I was now ready and allowing it.

I asked the question, *"What would it take for me to experience world peace?"* The answer I received was, *"World peace will occur when the basic needs of everyone are met, guaranteed, and; everyone has the opportunity to go higher, guaranteed."*

It's that simple. It's that complex.

That definition wasn't what I was expecting. Is it what you were expecting? And yet, to me, what really mattered was that I finally had the answer from God. It felt good, really good. It was truth about world peace. It arrived accompanied by a feeling from my soul that was all encompassing of my body. There was a certainty about it. It was accompanied by a sense of knowingness, that it was truth.

Now I had a place to start. It was a foundation to build on. Soon thereafter I received an answer to the question *"How will we do that?"* The answer is *"What is needed is not a change in* **circumstance** *but rather a change in* **consciousness**.*"*

The world has been working on changing **circumstances** for thousands of years, to no avail. How many humans would have shifted from changing **circumstances** to changing **consciousness** had they known that that was what was needed?

We have a worldwide consciousness, that it is someone else who is at fault for not having world peace, that what others are doing is causing the absence of world peace. This worldwide belief is mass consciousness creating what mass consciousness can.

You have taken the opportunity to join many others in changing your consciousness, automatically contributing to a mass consciousness shift, a consciousness of creating the opportunity of experiencing world peace.

We have the technology, knowledge and resources to experience world peace now. If everyone knew what world peace was we'd have it now. You can help them know that.

Everyone can contribute to guaranteeing that every person on earth has their basic needs met. Some of the basic needs that come to mind are: love, food, water, shelter, clothing and more. Everyone can also contribute to guaranteeing that every person on earth has the opportunity to go higher. Some things that come to mind here are: freedom that extends into being free to think what we choose to think without fear, no restrictions on asking and receiving and expressing what we've learned, and much more. When these lists are complete they will feel good.

According to our creator, there are two major changes in thinking that we are faced with making on our path to creating world peace. They are 1. God is Man made and 2. Man is God made.

Defining God

Most religions have defined God as something that God is but also as something that God is not. We humans have come up with numerous definitions of what God is and does. Each religion has its own definition. Some say God is all good and yet man should fear God. Many say God is everywhere and yet claim there is a hell where satan resides and God does not. This God is Man made.

Why on earth did man ever start defining God as something that God is not? When man did that thousands of years ago what was man's reason for doing so? Did man think that by defining God as something that God is not, that God would change to being that? Did man want God to change to something other than what God is? Do you want God to be something other than what God is?

Do you think man knows better what God should be than what God knows God should be? I believe that man did not want to change God from what God is but rather wanted to change man's thoughts about what God is.

In large part, man has succeeded, not in changing what God is, but in changing man's thoughts about what God is. Man succeeded by placing into man's mind thoughts not aligned with what God is.

Man must now choose again, to put new thoughts into man's mind, thoughts that align with what God is. The God that was, before man started defining God, is the God that man must align with again before world peace is possible.

Man Is God Made

Humans are **not** admiring their amazingly magnificent bodies as they should be. (An entire chapter earlier in this book is devoted to explaining the wondrously magnificent body.) They are not understanding that their body is love. Understanding that Man is God made is to fully understand that concept. Man is soul, body and mind, working together in harmony, unity and oneness. Man is love in soul - as that is what the soul is. Man is love in body in that the body is wondrously magnificent with God in it. Man is love in mind if man so chooses to fill his mind with love.

You achieved this new understanding earlier in this book. Help others to understand as well. Help them feel good and be a little better than they were before.

By filling the mind with love, and God is love, the mind joins the soul and body to be love. You don't just think love; you are love. Be love. You will then attract love. I did. I attracted Becky, my life partner, into my life in this way. I've attracted a better life into my life. Many more of my experiences now have love as a member. Yours will too. You are being love.

Try to be something. For example, try to be love. You cannot be love until you have experienced love. You cannot experience love until you know love. It must be in that order; know, experience, be. This is the holy trinity.

Try this! Know that 1. your soul is love; 2. your body is love; 3. your mind is love, as you are now filling your mind with experiences that have love as a member. The three parts of you that make you up, are each love. With the three parts of you that you are each being love, there is no other part of you left to not be love. You are love. Now, in this moment, experience that you are love. Now that you have experienced that you are love, you are being love. Know it. Experience it. Be it. From now on, when anyone says, *"Be love!"*, you can reply, *"I am."*

Now that you have changed your consciousness about **who you really are**, you are already a part of the consciousness change that is needed. You are being, or in the act of becoming, an instrument of world peace. You are on your path to participating in creating world peace.

God is Man made

The real God, the creator, the almighty, existed before man started making up their own man made God. Here are just a few of the differences.

- God is love. The God that man made up is to be feared.
- God does not judge. The God that man made up judges whether you sin and if you are going to hell.
- God is everywhere. The God that man made up is everywhere except in hell where the devil is.
- God created everything and everything God created was good. The God that man made up had God creating bad people who had to confess their sins.
- The real God said ask and you shall receive. The man-made God allowed prayer, but answers should be sought only from religious leaders.

Changing your mind from the fears that **man made up** about God to the love that God is is a change in consciousness. The soul knows and sends you those good feelings. The soul knows that God is not fear; that love and fear cannot occupy the same space; that God created everything and everything that God created was good;

that God is everywhere and everywhere is where fear cannot be. Fear does not exist except as thoughts and thoughts are made up constructs of the mind.

Fear is something which you are not. You can fill your mind with fear but you cannot fill your soul or your body with fear. For you to be fear you would need to fill your mind, your body and your soul with fear. Then you would be fear. Therefore, fear is something you cannot be. You can however be love.

When you get over your fear you will experience love. Once you get through experiencing fear, that which you are not, you will seek to experience love, that which you are.

War and peace are not opposites. War is an event, a circumstance. Peace is what you are **being**. Peace, love, joy, harmony, unity and oneness are all interchangeable words. All of them are what you are **being**, not what you are **doing**. War is something you are **doing**. Peace, a derivative of love, and war, a derivative of fear, cannot occupy the same space.

The mainstream news media and religions are instruments of war! They fill the mind with thoughts of fear. They avoid

discussion or inclusion of feelings to attain truth.

They choose to fill our minds with fear in an attempt to control our minds. By controlling our minds they attempt to control us. By controlling us they attempt to control circumstances. By controlling circumstances they fill our minds with fear. What they cannot control however is the **feeling experienced** with their deception.

Humans will make world peace happen when enough humans decide to make it happen. As with everything else, there is no desire that anyone holds for any other reason than that they believe they will feel better in the achievement of it.

A good feeling is never experienced while experiencing fear.

I believe I have become an instrument of world peace, partly because of writing this book. Join me in spreading the word about this book, by spreading the words, thoughts and ideas that are in this book. Introduce the world to the world of ICURY and you will change the world.

We humans are the only thing standing in the way of experiencing world peace. Nature, the environment, outer space, as well as everything else surrounding humans, are not standing in the way of humans experiencing world peace. Those things have no choice in the matter.

Imagine world peace! Picture it in your mind! World peace is certainly important enough to have each of us spend at least a few minutes thinking about it. We can all create our own vision of what world peace will look like.

Our vision will contain the good, the positive, the higher self. It will contain war if attaining or maintaining world peace is the only reason for the war. It will include feeding all the children on earth. It will not include people hurting other people, being mean to one another, wishing bad things on others, and so on. Our vision of world peace includes love, joy, peace, harmony, unity and oneness.

Happiness is a state of mind. Change your mind and you change your happiness. Like all states of mind, happiness produces itself in physical form. Think happiness and you become happy. Quit thinking happiness and happiness goes away. All states of mind reproduce themselves. Think angry thoughts and you become angry. Quit thinking angry thoughts and anger goes away. Think lonely thoughts and you become lonely. Quit thinking lonely thoughts and loneliness goes away.

Now take it to another level. Think world peace! It's easy to think happy thoughts because you know what happy is since you've experienced happy before in your life. It's easy to think angry thoughts since you've experienced anger in your life. It's easy to think lonely thoughts since you've experienced lonely in your life.

Think world peace! You find it much harder to think thoughts of world peace as you've not experienced that before. And nobody else on earth has experienced world peace either. It's time that changed. It's about to change.

You now know the truth about what it would take to experience world peace. You cannot work towards a goal of experiencing world peace unless you first know what that goal is. You now know that you can make world peace your goal and attain it.

To simply talk about world peace does not create world peace. To simply want world peace or to claim to work for world peace does not create world peace. These things have been done for centuries and the observable truth is that that has not worked. One could argue that we are no closer to world peace than the world was 100 years ago or 1,000 years ago. Look around and notice what you observe in the world today. There is chaos of one sort or another in every country on earth. Even nature is in chaos, not just here, but around the globe. Nature cannot be and will not be in chaos during world peace.

Many people have worked at creating world peace. Many people have worked to create world peace, as they envision world peace to be. The reason world peace didn't occur is that the people working at creating world peace were not actually working at creating world peace at all.

First and foremost, those people did not know what the true definition of world peace was. They did not ask God for the definition of world peace. If they asked, they did not get an answer. If they did ask and did get an answer, they did not recognize or pay attention to the answer or they did not act on it.

All along, God has known what it takes for us to experience world peace. All along God has been willing to tell us what world peace is. All along God has been telling us to ask. All along God has been telling us to ask and you shall receive. All along God has been waiting for us to wake up to this truth; to ask and you shall receive.

You have awakened to this truth and are consciously making changes to help you along your path.

We are on our way to make world peace happen. You will help make it happen. You can either be actively involved in creating world peace or you can be one of the inactive with doubts. If you choose to be inactive, you will have those doubts until the tipping point is reached when you will no longer have a choice but to be a part of experiencing world peace. This tipping point will occur when enough people have changed their consciousness to affect a mass consciousness change.

You're not going to feel hopeful until you're chasing after something that really matters to you. World peace matters to you and you are hopeful that you will experience world peace. You do not want to leave this world in chaos. You want this for your children, grandchildren, friends, relatives and associates to experience. It really matters to you and you will start chasing after it and in the process you will feel hopeful.

World peace is possible if we pay attention to ICURY and the rest of our special **feeling**

delivering friends. If it helps, name one of your butterflies too. Do what feels good.

My goal is to experience world peace. Many think it is impossible so why try. In many people's mind, traveling to the moon was impossible, but that was important enough to try and to succeed. World peace is very much more important than going to the moon.

Every nation needs to have a goal of world peace in place. Many nations spend a great deal of effort and money on war, preparing for war and paying for war.

Even with world peace there can be fighting and there can even be war, but both must only be to bring about or maintain world peace.

To be totally at peace within ourselves, everybody on earth needs to have that same opportunity.

In a world peace economy, you will not do things for personal profit but for personal growth, which will be your profit. Yet, profit in material terms will come to you as you become a bigger and grander version of who you are.

Today's culture is measured largely by how much honor, money, power and possessions we amass. In a culture of world peace, it will be measured by how much you cause others to amass.

Life will be about the highest quality giving vs the highest quality getting.

Nothing is more stimulating to humans than the prospect of peace. Peace is another word for love, or freedom, or joy, or truth or unity. These words comfort our soul, make sense in our minds, and reside in our body.

You could not experience a feeling of greater peace if you did not first experience peace in a lesser form. Greater cannot exist without that which is not greater. Have you experienced the greater? Do you want to?

Not wanting peace violates human nature – and that is the nature God gave us. You may not normally move towards a peace full world but you always naturally move towards a peace full world.

You are now part of the group, a group with a consciousness of belief that we are creating a peace full world. We, therefore, have a group consciousness which is far more powerful than the individual powers of the group. Consciousness is everything. Consciousness creates your experience. The power of group consciousness produces outcomes of unspeakable beauty. Grow the group.

I know you want a peaceful world. Start by contributing a joyful person to it. Joy is most fully and most rapidly experienced by giving it away.

Bring joy to another by reading this book to them. Some simply do not have the wherewithal to acquire and or read their own book. Until an audio version of this book is developed, reading to the blind allows you to bring joy to the blind. Read this book aloud and you will notice a greater impact than reading it in silence. Remember what you read earlier in this book: That which you think of, but thereafter never speak of, creates at one level. When you are reading out loud, you are speaking, and creating at another level.

I've read and reread this book many times in an effort to complete it to my satisfaction. While reading this book out loud with no one else around, I could sense a difference as it felt better than reading it in silence. I was creating at another level as you can too.

We live in a world where everyone can be a broadcaster. Computers, cell phones and the Internet are there to assist us. Spread the word. Phone your families. Text your friends. Share the word on forums and blogs. Using the Internet, and technology surrounding it, we can spread the word faster today than ever before.

We have the desire, the ability and the technology to create world peace faster than ever before. The desire, the ability and the technology to reach a massive amount of minds quickly is right in front of us. One has to believe that God saw this plan coming together and prepared it for us. Or prepared us for it.

We broadcasters must simply reach a tipping point in which our collective consciousness results in a shift in universal consciousness.

Do you fear becoming an instrument of peace? Be fear and you are being less of God as fear is that which God is not. Be love and you are being more of God as love is that which God is.

Be love and you will be fear-less. Become it. Be it. Feel the freedom. Freedom is not pure with the presence of fear.

Gratitude is a step anyone can take that yields immediate relief.

Pour yourself into yourself and see how wondrously magnificent you are.

Change your **come from** and you change your life. For example, I was going to meet my daughter. Previous meetings with her included anger. My thoughts are that it will be that way again this time. And it will be. I am and have been making it so. My come from is from anger. I noticed this, acknowledge it, and replaced the anger with love. I made my come from love, not just while I was going to meet her but while we were together. It changed my life and it changed my relationship with my daughter. When your thoughts and your actions are coming from love everything changes. It worked for me.

When you come from happiness, you do certain things because you are happy. This is opposed to, the old paradigm in which you did things that you hoped would make you happy.

When you come from wisdom you do certain things because you are wise, not because you are trying to get to wisdom.

When you come from love, you do certain things because you are love, not because you want to have love.

Everything changes when you **come from being** instead of **seeking to be**. You cannot get to being by doing. The way to get there is to be there. There is nothing you have to do to be happy. Be happy. You want to be wise. Be wise. You want to be love. Be love.

For you to start creating a meaningful relationship with God you must first stop fearing God. We've heard many times that blessed are the fearless for they shall know God. Start being fearless by discarding what you think you already know about God. God is not bad nor is God to be feared. Trash what others have told you about God being bad, judging or punishing you. Notice how you feel with your new thoughts as you enter into your own experience of God. Discard any guilt you may feel. Feeling good is you experiencing your soul communicating with you, telling you that you are on the right path. That is nothing to feel guilty about.

To summarize, I asked and I received. I have shared many of my questions, and many of the answers I received with you in this book. It feels good. Actually, it feels way better than good. I have also experienced a tremendous consciousness shift since starting this project. I can now say without doubt that I am love, that I am peace, that I am joy, that I am harmony, that I am unity, that I am oneness, and so much more. I simply **cannot not** be as God is in me and God is all that I am and so much more.

You can do all that I have done, and more. You can do all that I am doing, and more. You can be all that you are being, and more.

ICURY is the answer. Spell ICURY, out loud.

I – I

C – see

U – you

R – are.

Y – Why? And now you know Y.

Pay attention to your soul and to what ICURY is delivering to your body from your soul, and you will know Y you are, and Y you are here on earth. The opportunity for you to go higher has always been there. Now you know how to take advantage of that opportunity. You are going higher, and will continue to go much higher by your own choosing.

Thank you for reading ICURY. I did my best, with God's help, to make this the best book

I could. You undoubtedly realize by now, after reading this book, that I could not have put these words together without Gods help. Many paragraphs were changed several times until they felt good. In that light, I also need to thank my soul for sending those feelings.

God is happy that I wrote this book. I know this to be true because God is in me and I am happy that I wrote this book. God is also happy that you read this book. I know this to be true because God is in me and experienced my being happy that you read this book. Happiness is my response ability in action. You have response ability as well. How did you respond? Is God happy that you read this book? If so, you created that. If not, you created that. It is your response to reading this book. You, and only you, are response able for that.

Imagine a child asking you if he or she could get world peace as a birthday gift, and you could respond by saying, *"It's on its way."* How would you feel? How would that child feel? You are helping to make it happen.

Early on in this project God provided and helped me tremendously with rediscovering a note I had written and saved.

Remember this, it is not nearly so important how well a message is received as how well it is sent.
- How clearly
- How lovingly
- How compassionately
- How sensitively
- How courageously
- How completely

I referred to this message many times as I prepared my messages to you in this book. Kindly keep this in mind as you go about spreading the message of peace around the world.

This message also came to me: A good story should introduce you to a world you do not know and in that world you find yourself. I did.

Consciousness Shift Summary

You've experienced consciousness shifts while reading this book. Some you had before, some you learned and some are on their way.

God said a change in consciousness is needed to achieve world peace. You have made that change. You are creating world peace.

Body

You now fully understand that you have a wondrously magnificent body, full of love, full of peace, full of God. You are now taking conscious action, noticing your feelings and acting on them.

You now love your body with its trillions of points of consciousness. You know that when you love your body, you love God.

You don't just like your body, you love your wondrously magnificent temple. You don't just think it or believe it, but rather you know your body is love.

Soul

You now understand how important it was for you to shift from ignoring your soul to acknowledging the messages of truth sent by your soul to you in every moment.

You now realize that your soul holds your life plan and communicates that plan to you through feelings. You've become consciously aware of your feelings and have learned to consciously select thoughts that serve you on your life path.

You now know your soul is love, peace and truth. Your shift has you taking conscious actions of love.

Mind

You are developing conscious thought awareness and conscious thoughts of love. You're building unity of body, soul and mind. You've learned that harmony in you occurs only when you fill your mind with love so that your mind matches your soul and your body which are always filled with love.

You are consciously shifting your mind from being fear full to being love full. You are shifting from having mind, or mental, toughness to having soul, or feeling, toughness, moving from sheer determination and iron will to mindless allowing.

Body, Soul, Mind

Your soul was love from its very beginning. Your body was love from its beginning. They will always be love. Now you're consciously adding love to your mind, making all of you love.

Unity and Oneness

You've learned that you are unity and oneness with God, as to not be would deny your body and your soul.

You know that you are more in unity with God by continuing to consciously fill your mind with experiences of love.

The actions of your body, which your mind causes your body to do, are filled with love.

Your soul is one with God, simply by being, as it is filled with God.

Your body is one with God, simply by being, as it is filled with God.

Your mind is one with God, as you continue to fill your mind with love.

By consciously filling your mind with love, you become one with God

Harmony

You learned that when you have fear, love cannot be there, as love and fear cannot occupy the same space at the same time. You learned that harboring fear means you have a part of your mind working against your body and soul. You learned that fear only exists in your mind and removing fear from your mind removes it from you, from who you are being.

You learned that you, mind, body and soul, are in harmony when fear is replaced by love. You now have conscious thoughts and actions to create harmony in you.

Consciousness

You now more fully understand conscious awareness, conscious thought, conscious action and unconscious reaction.

You are consciously being a higher self. You are better than you were before.

Ask and you shall receive: You continue to grow by asking the source, God, creator, for answers while trusting that you'll receive and allow answers on your path to moving higher.

You're asking many more questions, not covered in this book, leading to peace filled education, business, government, religion, medical and many other areas of life.

You've shifted from asking for peace to creating peace, by being peace.

Experiences

You've learned one of the biggest lessons of your life. You now know that your life is simply a series of experiences, one followed by another, and since you create every one of your experiences, you create your life. By creating your experiences, each with love as a member, you create a life of love. You are being love. You are love experienced.

Source

You have a consciousness of treating others, this book and every other book as a source and treating God as the Source.

You

You have a consciousness that everyone is entitled to, has a right to, feel good and that they are each, individually, response-able to make that happen for themselves. You now know that it starts with you having a consciousness of building inner peace, all the while knowing that by building inner peace you are building world peace. The good feelings you experience have you being cause of creating and attracting more peace.

Massive Shift

Never before in the history of this planet has mankind been more blessed with the tools, technology and know-how to spread God consciousness around the globe, easily and quickly. It's like God has been readying the world for the massive consciousness shift we are creating.

Birthing World Peace:

You are now rightfully enjoying being an instrument of world peace.

We now know what world peace is and how we will achieve it. We know that this is what God wants for each and every one of us.

Your love of everyone and everything is a love of God as God is everywhere and God is in everything.

You now treat your wondrously magnificent body as the temple it is. You love your body.

You now cherish your soul as the guiding power on your life path. You love your soul.

You flood your mind with thoughts and experiences of love. You love your mind.

You love you. You know that when you love you, you love God.

You know that you, mind, body and soul are the creation machine God intended you to be.

You know that when you are peace or are creating a peaceful moment you are creating a peaceful world.

You know that by creating one love experience after another, we are collectively enjoying creating world peace, now in its infancy.

By consciously creating one love experience after another, you are creating world peace. You are part of the mass consciousness shift needed to create it. Thank you.

You are wondrous magnificence.

Book Orders

By the time you read this, the English version of ICURY will be available in paperback and Kindle formats at the Amazon.com bookstore

Please visit www.PeacePreserve.com for the latest information about and the availability of ICURY in additional languages and formats.

Disclaimer

I acknowledge that if you don't believe in God, the likelihood of you becoming an instrument of peace will be pretty slim. I would, however, warn you that you may not understand the power of love others have over you, your thoughts, your beliefs, your mind.

I do not make any representation or promise regarding the effects or outcome of your celebration as you experience world peace.

I do not assume any responsibility for any declining medical needs, improved health conditions, joyful life events or situations you may have in the future.

The information received herein should not in any way be used as a substitute for advice from God.

Those participating in the creation of world peace need not be emotionally stable or of sound mind.

Participants and their heirs, representatives, successors and assigns, release and waive any and all claims they now have or may have in the future in connection with the joyous celebrations of world peace.

My ideas about world peace may be borrowed, used, copied, recorded, reproduced, adapted, altered, modified, taught, simplified, etc. in any way with the consent of God.

All results are final. No refunds. When you become love, you cannot turn back. Love is addictive. Once you receive it, it is yours. Once you give it, you attract more, and give move, and attract more.

Because of your new awareness of who you are being, you and only you are responsible for the heightened vibrational energy you will develop by stating your new beliefs out loud. The spoken belief is your word in action. Action is a higher creative power than thought or word alone.

Any no-shows or missed appointments with God are missed opportunities. Sorry, but no refunds. You cannot re-live something you have not lived. Pay attention or you'll miss out on choosing a path in your life plan.

Emergency appointments with God are never needed. God is always listening. God operates on a case-by-case basis, and treats you as the special case you are. You just aren't the only special case God is dealing with.

For those who have chosen to set up an ongoing, moment by moment, habit of listening to God, beware of dramatic changes in your continually improving life.

Please note that it may be harder to drop out of the habit of listening than it was to join the practice.

God does not offer a refund to those who feel they are receiving too many answers, too much love or joy or peace.

God offers only a lifetime subscription of love in your body and in your soul. No guarantee or subscription is available for your mind or it would negate the free will you were given to fill your mind, by yourself, with whatever you choose to fill it with.

You may pay a high price for not filling your mind with love and joy and peace and harmony and unity and oneness.

You are responsible for your love, for being love and for spreading love. You are a human being love.

Made in the USA
Lexington, KY
16 June 2017